NATU

CW00518163

POWER

Inspiring Nature-Infused
Short Stories

By

Dr Lennon Foo

For Devon and Toren,
with their journey ahead of them

For You, the eternal student and teacher of Life.

For my dear friend
Evangelos, the BIGGEST small
basketball player I know!

With Gratitude,
Lennon Sept 2011

CONTENTS

ENJOY

LEADERSHIP

SUCCESS

ACKNOWLEDGEMENTS

I have to start by thanking my sons, Devon and Toren. You keep me young and playful. Thank you for showing me how to look at the wondrous world through innocent and wholesome eyes again. You are a great teacher of simple and profound gratitude. You are proof that age is just a number and everyone has a lesson to teach. Thank you for reminding me how limitless our genius and powers can be. Thank you for showing me how to live.

I will be eternally grateful to my parents, aka Mummy and Papa. Allowing me to breathe in this world with independence and supporting the way I choose to live with no judgement or prejudice is more than I can ever ask. Thank you and I love you so much.

My amazing sister, Shennon, who provided a sense of belonging for me all these years abroad. You have taken care of me more than I have done so for you and, for that, I am grateful you are my blood.

Special thanks to Uncle Edward (Tuagu) for being a strong support, believing in me and my journey. Your achievement amongst others in my extended family reminds me I have come from a family of greats.

Also, to Uncle Han Cheong (Jigu) who believed and invested in me not too long ago. Thank you and I will show you that you have great investment acumen.

Never forgetting Uncle Andrew Cheng, Ong Lay Hong (Qiyi), and Kuang who also saw the potential in me. Thank you and you ROCK as a family!

Thank you, Uncle Reto, for your financial help not too long ago. You are like the foreign uncle I never had.

Through the ups and downs of the last two decades of my life, Carol and Martin King, you have been there for me. A solid rock that I never expected in a foreign land. Somehow, you always saw the good in me. Thank you for taking care of me, celebrating my successes, and supporting me through my tribulations.

I feel luckier than Charlie for I have not three but four Angels in my life. Despite thousands of miles separating us, we nurtured and invested in our friendship, resulting in something special and timeless. Thank you, Beatrice Yuen, Linda Lim, Lynette Koh, and Adeline Sim for our laughter, tears, and joy for nearly three decades. I am truly blessed.

No man is an island. I would not be able to do what I do without my fantastic Amity Team. They are the most incredible group of people I know. One, for doing what they do, and two, for putting up with me. Thank you for allowing me to lead you and teaching me daily.

Thank you, my inspired reader, who chose to pick this book up and read it. I believe there is an under-running current of connection between all people. By sharing our thoughts, we collectively become stronger and better. Thank you for strengthening me.

Introduction

What does a Dalmatian looking into a mirror, a macaw stretching his wings, a baby learning to walk, and bamboo have in common?

Seemingly nothing, except ...

Are you struggling to find the good in you, physically and emotionally? You see yourself and feel bad. You are uncomfortable in your own body.

Do you feel like there is more to you than what you are right now? You know you have it in you. However, something is holding you back. Something is eluding you.

Have you ever failed in something despite having multiple attempts and given up? You tried so many times and did not succeed. You felt it is not meant to be.

Do you feel frustrated after putting in so much effort but still did not see any results? Despite all the energy, time, and money you have invested in a skill, a job, a relationship, you had nothing to show for it. The results obtained did not match the amount of effort put in.

I know I have, and I do. Nico, the Dalmatian, will show you your magic. Sunny, the macaw, will stretch your mind. A baby will remind you of your persistence leading to success. Learn from a growing bamboo why your results are seemingly elusive.

First of all, I would like to thank you for getting this book. I also wish to congratulate you on investing in yourself, not many do that. I may not know you personally, but I know of someone like you.

What if I told you that the above beliefs are all lies?

Imagine being able to feel good all the time, learning there is more to you than you can ever imagine, being able to understand that success takes time and you are actually on the right path.

In this book, you will be shared profound lessons in life using life's simple occurrences as an effective teacher. You will learn about Growth, Challenges, Enjoyment, Leadership, and Success. You will find insights that have eluded you for so long. Its simple-to-use and easy-to-understand stories and principles will guide and inspire you to become the better version of yourself. You will learn that the knowledge is already within you.

In my continuing journey as a father and business owner, I have shared many challenges that life brings, just like you. I have fallen and failed many times. However, there has been moments of triumph and success too. I have been fortunate to have multiple events to have happened to me, both good and bad, allowing me to grow from the challenges and enjoy the wondrous beauty of life.

I would like to share what I have learnt with you. Each Nature-woven short story will bring a specific point. It allows easy understanding and simple lessons that serves as a reminder in your daily undertakings. At the end of each story, there is a question to evoke your thoughts and provoke your status quo. Sometimes all the inspiration you need is found around and inside you. Please be sure to commit to the action tip too!

Use this book as a guide. Don't just read it, be sure to use it. You can dip and dive to which story resonates most with you at the time. Or you can read it from front to back if you prefer.

Life is too good to be spent on regret, wasted on sadness and unfulfilled due to unexpressed potential. You are more than who or what you think you are. Join me in the exploration of your wonderful life. Let's start with something that we all do physically and mentally, Growing ...

Growing

STRETCHING YOUR POTENTIAL

Sunny is a four-month-old blue-gold macaw that has been hand-reared. He stands proud on his favourite cherry branch in his outdoor aviary. The sun is shining, and the air is still. He has stood many times there before looking at the 15-foot drop before him. He shifts his weight from his right foot to his left foot, swaying like a pendulum. He squawks gently to himself. His wings had grown immensely in the last eight weeks. He bobs his head up and down and stretches his wings from time to time, as if saying, "Should I or should I not? Are my wings ready to fly or shall I wait longer?" He sees a fully grown macaw flying from branch to branch. He turns back to see what is below him.

IN LIFE, YOU WERE BORN PERFECT. A gentle breeze picks up and it seemed to bring Sunny the confidence he needs. It seemed to remind him that he is a majestic blue-gold macaw and was meant to soar in the skies, not scrabble around the ground or climb trees with his claws and beak like a flightless bird. His eye glistened. He stretched his wings, stepped off the branch, and flew a few metres before landing slightly clumsily on a low branch about ten metres away. He stood up and squawked, as if proudly saying, "Did you see that? I flew! I am incredible!" And just like that, in those few minutes, Sunny had achieved something he did not before and became someone he was not before. In short, he had stretched his potential.

In life, you were born perfect. Even with any congenital conditions, you were still born with a perfect set of energy, ability, and soul that is unique to you. The potential in you is infinite. You learned to walk without guidance, lessons, or courses. You learn to talk by mimicking all around you. You learn how to write, count, and achieve goals through lessons, determination, and diligence. Sure, you may have had teachers and mentors who taught and mentored but it was you who did it. With your innate ability and the support from the environment, you did it.

Maybe you have achieved something amazing like completing your studies, obtaining a degree, or becoming the parent you always wanted to be. Perhaps it was simply improving your health or lifestyle, like quitting smoking, escalating your fitness, or eating healthily consistently. All this involved you stretching your potential to become the better version of you.

I recall being an average student in school. Consistently over almost 10 years, the teachers' reports were similar, along the lines of "He is capable of better work", "There is more that he can give" or "I can see the potential in him". It was always saying how bright I was but not "blossom" yet. There are people who live their entire lives 'having potential' but not achieving what they could fully achieve if they had realised and stretched that potential. They did not become better, or much less, the best versions of themselves.

Einstein said, "Great spirits have always encountered

violent opposition from mediocre minds". Have you ever felt that when you want to do something incredible, someone else (usually your family or close friend) will try to talk you down? They may say things like, "That is impossible", "That cannot be done" or "Why do want to do that?" It is almost as if you had gone mad. That, unfortunately, is common because you are operating at a different level of understanding and awareness from them. You may decide to persist on and achieve your goals, improving yourself when doing so, or you may decide to give up and agree with them that you are being 'impractical' or 'unreasonable'.

An alternative interpretation would be to say you possess a great spirit and a mediocre mind. You are born with a great spirit that intuitively knows what is right and wrong (for you), what your potential is, and what your greatest dreams and burning desires are. No one else was involved in that thinking. Unfortunately, your environment, including your parents, family, friends, teachers, and all things and everyone who makes up your surroundings, has influenced your thinking and affected your mediocre mind. So, your logical (but mediocre) mind (that is wholly made up of your past experiences from the environment you are in) thinks it knows best and tries to reason with your sovereign spirit. That is a mistake. Your spirit is the true wholesome you that you see and speak to in the dark and stillness of the night. It knows things that you cannot explain. Its knowledge is Infinite. On the other hand, your mind's knowledge and information is Finite as it is limited to only what you have been exposed to.

You have to learn to understand that you are no
your thoughts. You are more than that. Learn to listen
to your spirit and seek guidance from within.
Greatness is an inside game, not an outside one.
Learn NOT to believe yourself when you are talking
yourself out of something. Learn NOT to listen to
yourself when you are saying it is too difficult or it is
impossible. Potential unexpressed turns into pain. In
twenty years' time, you will regret the things you did
not do more than the things that you did.

Sunny believed in something he thought he could do
but had never done. As a result, he flew. What about
you?

Question: What would you do if you had no fear?

Action Tip: Do at least one thing out of your routine
daily.

It is sad to see a child being afraid of the dark.

It is even worse to see a grown-up being afraid of the light."

– Anon

TO BE OR NOT TO BE,

HAVE YOU GOT THE ANSWER?

Sue called out to Kari, a beautiful five-year-old black and tan Doberman, "Come back! Time to go!" Kari stopped in her tracks. Her ears were pricked straight up, her body stiffened and faced the rabbit that was bounding away but her head tilted back to her guardian. The sun was shining, and the breeze was gentle. You can almost see the thought process going on in Kari's mind, "Should I chase, or should I head back? The rabbit is fun to chase, and I am sure I will get him this time, not like the last time but I know there is a delicious treat waiting for me if I listen! Am I going to be Kari, the one who caught the rabbit, or Kari, the dog who gets her treat?" In the end, Kari watched the rabbit run away and started to run back to Sue joyfully, stretching her powerful legs and arching her supple spine, almost salivating thinking about her tasty reward. Life is indeed good!

> BE SURE YOU MAKE ALL DECISIONS THAT AFFECT YOU IN ANY WAY AT ALL COSTS.

Every day, you make choices. From what to eat and wear to deciding if you want to get out of bed or not!

11

When you were young, you were taught right and wrong, first by your parents, and then the lesson was extended to the classroom where your teachers taught ideas like reading, writing, arithmetic, and much more. They taught you the right way of reading or the wrong way of adding (how 2 + 2 is not 5), etc. This lesson of right or wrong is further supplemented and reinforced by society with laws, social norms, and regulations.

Sometimes, it is easy to think life is made up of right and wrong choices. It can be challenging as you do not want to be wrong, so you feel like you have to make the right choice every time. If you do not and make a wrong choice, somehow you have done the wrong thing and are letting someone down (either someone else and/or yourself).

To extend that thought further, it can be almost paralyzing to make choices in fear of choosing the wrong one. Examples include what subject to study, what job to take, should I marry that person or not, should I take this course, where should I live, what car should I buy, should I go to that party, should I buy life insurance and many more. You get the gist. There are so many 'important' decisions to make in life that it is sometimes easier to do nothing and 'let nature takes its course'. Over time, the decision may be taken away or made for you.

What if there was an alternate way of thinking? What if instead of viewing decisions or choices as right or wrong, you simply see them as actions and consequences? There are no right or wrong decisions or choices, only consequences for each one that you make. (Even not making a choice is a decision. And there are certainly consequences for that.)

Remember, there are no right or wrong choices, only the consequences differ. That is simply it. There is no need to assign right or wrong, only understanding and accepting the result. Perhaps the most important aspect of this is that you are better off making the choice than having the decision taken out of your hand. Once there is not the guilt of 'making the wrong choice', you should just simply decide and observe the consequence. You either find the result favourable or you don't. If you do, repeat it. If you don't, learn from it. Sometimes you win, sometimes you learn.

There are two kinds of decisions worth focusing on.

HARD ONES because you know that whatever you choose is possibly the wrong path. Hard decisions are hard because you have competing priorities. Hard decisions that happen often are probably a sign that the system you're relying on isn't stable, which means that the thing you did last time might not be the thing you want to do this time.

EASY ONES because it probably means that you've got a habit going. And an unexamined habit can easily become a rut, a trap that leads to digging yourself deeper over time.[1]

Every time you make a decision, you learn, you grow, and you become more than what you were before making that decision. Be sure to grow. To find your

---

[1] Credit to Seth Godin

best self, you must lose your weak self. That only happens through relentless improvement, continuous reflection, and ongoing self-excavation.

Be sure you make all decisions that affect you in any way at all costs. It is your life. Make it yours and not others. If you do not have a plan for your life, you can be sure that someone else does!

Kari chose her reward instead of the rabbit. What do you choose?

Question: What is the most compelling idea that you have? Are you making decisions to realize that idea?

Action Tip: Make fast decisions. Fail fast and learn faster.

"The tragedy of life is not death but what we let die inside of us while we live."

– Robin Sharma

WHO IS TEACHING WHO?

It was Lizzie and Max's third obedience class. Max is a handsome but stubborn one-year-old Lurcher. Lizzie was teaching Max how to listen to commands like 'sit' and 'heel'. Max was having nothing of it. After 15 minutes, Max was well and truly bored. He was fidgeting, his eyes were darting elsewhere and searching for more interesting things to do. Lizzie kneeled down to Max's level and spoke sternly to him, "Max, come. Listen to me." Max simply stared back, with a blank expression, almost saying, "Seriously, I have had enough. This is boring. Let's go to the river instead!" The face-off continued until Max slipped the lead and Lizzie chased after him, swearing that he was the most disobedient dog ever.

> EVERYBODY'S FAVOURITE BUSINESS IS THEIR OWN BUSINESS.

Have you ever tried to teach someone, and nothing was getting in? Or explain something to someone in vain? No matter how hard you tried or regardless of the technique used, it was like talking to a brick wall, where even a tree stump had more response. It is moments like these you need to seriously consider what you are even doing. There are times when you try so hard and it is usually because the topic at hand is so important to you that you feel extremely frustrated when the other party is not reciprocating. Sometimes, it is something you know that will benefit the other party immensely which is why you try so hard. But they just do not seem to get it or even care.

This may be when you are trying too hard to teach instead of trying to learn. The most outstanding teacher is the most outstanding student. It is when you empty your cup, have no expectations, and seek first to understand before expecting to be understood that you allow the other party to be open to receive. Everyone's favourite business is their own business. When they realise that you want to understand them and allow them to express their feelings, emotions, and thoughts, then they will listen to what you have to say. After all, what you are telling them is 'your business' and there is no reason why they should feel obliged to listen in the first place.

Some may learn like you, many have their own way of learning and processing information that may be vastly different from you. When you are explaining something to someone or training your beloved pet, a simple question to ask would be, "Who is learning from who?" or "Who is training who?" You may find that, despite thinking that you are the one doing the explaining to someone and that person has something to learn from you, the reality is actually you have been given the opportunity to learn from them. They are teaching you how to speak to them. Similarly, when you are 'training' your pet, understand that your pet may actually be training you instead. He may be telling you that you may have to change your method, something else needs to happen before he listens or, simply, he is not interested as he does not see any benefit in that training.

In future, before you feel exasperated because you are failing to get your point across, ask yourself if you have been learning from them or have you just been simply bulldozing your point across. If you are not prepared to listen or to learn, it is likely that they will do the same, not listen or learn. If you persist, you will find only frustration, stress, and, likely, failure despite your best and earnest intentions.

Instead, may I suggest that you 'forget' (temporarily) your original idea and just completely open your mind, heart, and soul so you are in a completely 'receiving' (rather than 'transmitting') mode to them and see what they want. If possible, fulfil their dreams and goals first. If not possible, at least listen and seek to understand why they have expressed those dreams. Only then should you attempt to make your point. The best teachers are the best students. And likewise, the best students make the best teachers.

After Max has ran his course around the river for 20 minutes, Lizzie only took a single try to get him to sit and heel. They had both learnt from each other. Lizzie had to learn first as she was the one who initiated the teaching.

Question: What holds you back from fully listening to the other party?

Action Tip: Practise listening in full without interruption, only nodding your head even if you do not agree.

"Cooperativeness in conversation is achieved when you show that you consider the other person's ideas and feelings as important as your own. Starting your conversation by giving the other person the purpose or direction of your conversation, governing what you say by what you would want to hear if you were the listener, and accepting his or her viewpoint will encourage the listener to have an open mind to your ideas."

– Dale Carnegie

CHANGING COLLARS

I watched as Patricia removed a well-used collar from Gnome, her Giant Schnauzer's neck, and replaced it with a brand-new personalized collar. She passed me the old collar and said, "He has had this collar for almost two years. It is worn out now. I tend to replace his collar every 18 months. I wonder if he knows the difference." Gnome had wandered away with his nose to the ground, focused and oblivious to the surroundings. The two of us are not convinced that he feels there was much of a difference to the change.

{ MOST PEOPLE ARE ADDICTED TO THEIR STRUGGLES. }

In life, change is the only constant. Even if you felt exactly the same as yesterday, something has invariably changed as, in the past day, you may have received a new stimulus, been exposed to a new concept, spoke to someone, or simply grew older.

Sometimes, the change is large enough to be perceived clearly, like choosing to start a new habit, job, relationship, or finding out something that dramatically changes your life like someone expressing his or her feelings for you, losing your job, getting pregnant, and many more. In those changes, how do you react to them? Do you take them in your stride, embracing every little bit of feeling and emotion that comes with it? Or do you try to ignore them, even denying them at times?

When change happens to you, something profound may happen, depending on your reaction. When you choose to ignore it or deny it, you remain the same … or do you? Let's consider the opposite. If you choose to completely embrace the change, not only accepting the physical aspects of it but also embracing the emotional portions, it becomes much more. It ceases to be merely a change in your knowledge, your environment, or your emotions, it actually presents the opportunity that allows you a change in your identity. And that, to some, is hard and often the reason why they may choose to ignore, resist, or deny it.

Humans are creatures of comfort. Once you have found comfort in a way of being, having expertise in some skill, or happy at your present state, it *almost* makes no sense to change that or give it all up for some unknown thing. That is just plain logic.

For some, it may not even be an ideal situation that they are comfortable in. They just simply have gotten used to that way of living that any change (even for the better) may be challenging and scary for them. They are addicted to their struggles. The fear of an identity change to something new and unfamiliar, even if it may mean an improvement in their lives, is too much and they would rather stick to their difficult but familiar life and self-identity. They have a fear of success.

Well, I did say "almost". If you thrive on changes, you may belong to one of two groups (and arguably, they are the same). You may enjoy the possibilities of the unknown, knowing that better things may happen, or your situation is so bad that anything else may seem to be an improvement. You may understand that you are not your thoughts. Any change in your life is a change and may contain the possibility of improvement. You also know that anything less than an identity shift or change will not allow you to become a better version of yourself if you are not able to shed the old self.

Next, you know that any change is potentially exciting, even more exciting to you than anyone else who does not see the possibilities. You enjoy changes that obviously improves your life but especially relish those that bring new challenges, as you know that it is this type that, when you have overcome them, you would have brought about not only an improvement in your life but also an improvement in your self-identity. This type of change is truly transformational, not just transactional.

For example, when you succeed in completing a course, the change would be that you have worked hard and succeeded as a result. However, if you had failed and taken it upon yourself to improve, try again and succeed, your change would be much more than just succeeding.

Gnome is oblivious to his new collar. What about you? When a change happens in your life, do you embrace it and allow it to change your identity to possibly improve or do you still wear the collar of your previous life?

Question: What specific emotion or memory holds you back from allowing yourself to experience something new?

Action Tip: Remember that you are not your thoughts. Allow yourself to fail for you will be given the opportunity to grow.

"The old you must die before the better you can be born."

THROUGH THE LOOKING GLASS

Nico, an eight-year-old male Dalmatian, has an interesting habit. He loves looking at the mirror. He would peek into the full-length mirror in his guardian's bedroom and then run downstairs to the hallway only to steal another glance into another full-length mirror there. Sometimes, he would only look, stay a few seconds, and run away only to return to repeat the process. At other times, he would stare for a few minutes in silence, occasionally cocking his head and adjusting his posture, as if thinking, "Who is that dog in there? Why is he looking at me and keeping his distance? Why is he not playing with me? Why does he get so animated at times and have no response at other times? Why does he look interested but does not engage? Why does he bark at me but I hear nothing?"

> IT IS NOT WHAT YOU SHOUT TO THE WORLD THAT MATTERS BUT THE CONSTANT WHISPERS YOU SAY TO YOURSELF THAT HAS THE MOST PROFOUND EFFECT.

Does Nico realize it is his reflection? Does he know the dog in the mirror is the physical image of himself? Is he aware that the capacity of emotion and movement of that dog is confined to his own capacity of emotion and movement? Is he self-aware? Are you self-aware?

What do you see when you look in the mirror? Do you like what you see? When you look in the mirror, what you see is your physical image. Every hair, expression, and nuances in your body are you. That is the physical instrument you have to reflect on your environment and the outside world. To a certain extent, it is a paradox. You can't really change the way you look (not instantaneously anyway!) or how others perceive you physically, but it is under your control how you want to be perceived. There are two important people in your life that will look, have an opinion, and judge you whether you like it or not. They are *yourself* and *others*.

Interestingly, by convincing one of them, you usually convince the other to come to the same conclusion. When you look in the mirror, are you able to accept, appreciate, and love what you see in its entirety and push past the physical image, delve deeper inside and accept, appreciate, and love what you cannot see in the mirror? Do you ask the same questions that Nico asks? When you look into the polished reflective glass, do you ask, "Who is that person in there? Why is (s)he looking at me and keeping her/his distance? Why is she/he not playing with me? Why does she/he get so animated at times and have no response at other times? Why does she/he look interested but does not engage? Why does she/he shout at me but I hear nothing?"

How do you feel when you look into the mirror? Do you only use it to put your make up on or to shave?

When you are not doing physical acts that require the mirror, do you look into it and just focus on who you see inside? How do you feel then? Are you complimentary of yourself, thinking, "Damn, I see myself as Nature intended and I feel good!" or critically thinking, "I do not like what I see and I feel horrible"? How do you feel? What is the dialogue you have with yourself? It is not what you shout to the world that matters but the constant whispers you say to yourself that has the most profound effect.

You are born perfect, exactly as Nature intended. Over time, you may have developed or acquired challenges like losing a limb, having a health condition, or experienced great loss/developed immense pain. Still, that is exactly as Nature intended. Everyone has different histories to tell but also possesses the same story to live for. Everything is exactly how it should be. Any perceived shortcomings like "too fat, too skinny, too short, too tall, not good looking enough, nose too big, nose too small, skin too rough, skin too delicate, too hairy, not enough hair" (you get the gist) is nothing compared to a fracture of your mind, the weakening of your emotions or the amputation of your soul. Learn how to preserve your mind, fortify your emotions, and escalate your soul for that is truly more important than what you see in the mirror.

There is an exercise that you can do.

Find a quiet spot and look into a mirror (a small face mirror would suffice but when you are braver and for a greater effect, use a full-length mirror). When you do so, really focus on each of your body parts that you can see. Get granular on this. Examine every square inch of your face and your body in detail. As you do so, think to yourself, "That's not too bad, that's enough, that's good, that's ok." If you are braver (or more advanced), start thinking, "That's beautiful, I have got great parts! I have bits of me that are unique and no one else has them!"

After you have done that (the next step is more fun and challenging), learn how to look beyond the looking glass. Still looking into the mirror, now look into your self-image, your mind, heart, and soul. For your mind, get in tune with your thinking. What are your thoughts? Acknowledge, understand, and accept them. For your heart, calibrate your feelings. How are you feeling? Recognize, embrace, and love them. For your soul, purify your essence. Remember your life force, your magic, and your gifts.

You have to learn how to love what you see in the mirror and beyond. You may start with only a few minutes in the beginning. That is usually how long most people can tolerate themselves! Over time, you may extend it longer, even up to half-hour or more! This is not being narcissistic. This is being one with yourself. The reality is that, if done properly, it will instil even greater humility in you and your appreciation of the world.

You will learn the joy of being friends with yourself, loving yourself like a life partner, and, in return, the world will do the same to you. You will become your greatest friend and lover and, subsequently, become a great friend and lover. You are unique. You are magical. You are enough. You will become like Nico, the bouncy Dalmatian!

Question: List three of your favourite body parts.

Action Tip: Find out what your loved one loves most about you.

"Stand in your own space and know that you are there."

UNFAIR ADVANTAGE

It was the annual fete at Belstone. The much-awaited dog race is the most anticipated event of the day. There were five liver and white Springer Spaniels tugging at their leads, seven tricoloured Jack Russell Terriers yelping with their high-pitched barks, and two beautiful spotty Dalmatians present for the race. In addition, there were about 25 other dogs of all shapes and sizes, including Shih Tzus, Pugs, and a lanky Boston Terrier, rearing to go at the start line. The air smelt of popcorn and hog roast. The lure was prepared with an experienced organiser walking past all the dogs allowing them to sniff it, only to increase the madness and mayhem of the already excited hounds. The finish line is about 80 metres away across the luscious green grass. With the lure prepared, the stage was set. The referee blew the foghorn and the hounds were released.

> REMEMBER THAT YOU ARE A PRODUCT OF CENTURIES OF CHANCE AND EVOLUTION.

At the 10-metre post, all dogs were more or less equal. At the 30-metre post, the toy dog breeds were left behind and a Dalmatian was leading with four Springers hot on her heels. This close race continued until the 50-metre post when, out of the blue, a red flash zoomed past all the leading dogs and reached the finish line before any dog had passed the 60-metre post. This red flash was a two-year-old Saluki. He is considered the world's second-fastest dog (after the Greyhound). His long legs, aerodynamic body shape, and supple spine are his unfair advantages. There was just no way the rest of the dogs could compete with him in this instance. He owned the game.

What is your unfair advantage? Are you maximising your unfair advantage to help you in life? Are you using it in your daily undertakings including your studies, work, relationships, and in yourself? One thing we all have in common is that we are unique. There is no one exactly the same as you. Your DNA, environment, experiences, mind, and soul are exclusive, completely different from others. You possess at least one unfair advantage over others. Some have compassionate souls, some have photographic memories, some are exceedingly detailed in their dealings, and some may have a flair for languages. Have you discovered yours? If you have, are you making the most of it to help you succeed in life?

Remember that you are a product of centuries of chance and evolution. Your ancestors were one of the few that survived the wars, natural disasters, and calamity. A unique sperm, out of the billions and billions, met an egg, out of so many eggs and cycles, to form a fertilised embryo, which, against all odds, developed into a foetus that resulted in you. Do you see what a miracle you are? In this complexity of chances and events, a unique you is formed. Are you still in any doubt that you are as special as you can be and there is no one else like you in the world? By extension, somewhere, somehow, you must possess at least one unique unfair advantage over everyone else on this planet. Have you discovered yours? Are you cultivating it to allow you to rock your world and lift everyone up around you by doing so?

Michael Phelps is double-jointed (allowing a greater range of movement), has a larger lung capacity (12 litres compared to the usual six litres), born with a longer torso than legs (making it ideal for swimming), and possesses size 14 feet (like flippers!). These are his unfair advantages over any other swimmer even before skills, coaching, and techniques are implemented! Michael Jordan's unfair advantage is his drive to succeed at all costs. He wasn't the tallest basketball player and not necessarily the fastest, however, no one else had as much drive as he did, and he was described as playing at a 'different' level. If he was competing at a different level, there is no competition.

So, know that you are special and possess at least one (or more) unfair advantage. Make sure you discover and cultivate it to allow it to smash your world with brilliance and success. You are BEAUTIFUL and YOU KNOW IT!

Question: What is one trait that had allowed you to see or do something no one else could accomplish or experience?

Action Tip: Ask your friend what is your most annoying trait. It may turn out to be your advantage!

"All personality traits have their good side and their bad side. But for a long time, we've seen introversion only through its negative side and extroversion mostly through its positive side."

– Susan Cain

COVID 1:

LEARNING FROM WITHIN

In the midst of COVID-19 pandemic, guidelines, advices, and regulations have been suggested, recommended, and, in some situations, imposed. Due to the degree of uncertainty and unknown about the virus, these guidelines, advices, and regulations change often.

As you face the unknown, it is common to feel FEARFUL. The Fear of Death, the Fear of Poverty, the Fear of Ill Health, the Fear of Loss of Love, and the Fear of Criticism are easily manifested in this situation. The outcome is that you may start to criticise, comment, become extremely opinionated, point fingers, and create negative feelings which do not necessary help matters.

At a launch of a famous artist's newest art piece, there were numerous theories on how the artist sourced his inspiration. Theories spun around his muse, his feelings, his current stage in life, his parents, his past, his depression, his happiness, and many more. When asked, the artist said that it was drawn when he was drunk, and he actually did not know where he got the inspiration from. What he felt was interpreted was

> FEAR IS THE MIND KILLER.

not his canvas but rather, the critics. The personality of each critic was revealed more than his art.

Many people have opinions about everything. Some like to voice them. Have you wondered why? Is it because they feel their thoughts need to be expressed? Or if they keep silent, no one notices them? Maybe they like to feel important? Perhaps it is their underlying need to connect? (I am aware that by writing this, I am also voicing my opinion!)

Usually, the deeper feeling may be tied to one or more of the Fears listed above. When you feel fearful, you take action. It could be flight, fight or freeze, sometimes you even fidget. Your mind becomes clouded. Fear is the mind killer. A killer virus on the loose, taking lives and disrupting your perceived normal lives, can be a potent catalyst for you to spin out of control. What has happened is this event has brought some form of fear that has originally resided in you out to light.

Despite everyone's perfect intentions, the execution will always be flawed. For every action (or inaction) taken, there will always be pros and cons. The world will NEVER agree collectively on anything. When you insist on making your point heard, it risks it being pointless. No one ever wins in an argument, regardless of outcome.

Instead, you can learn from this. No opinions are needed. You can choose to be extremely grateful for this crisis has allowed you the opportunity to grow. When you overcome this event (and you will, for no virus will wipe humanity from the face of the earth), you would have grown. Mistakes will be made, breakthroughs will be found, and what will certainly happen is that you would have learned something. The question is what. Some will learn how much they've lost, others will learn what truly matters, and all will learn more about themselves. Let yourself be mindful with your thoughts. Thoughts are truly things.

Keep safe, keep sane, and keep your immune system healthy. Healthy minds are essential for healthy bodies. Guard your mind from negative and toxic thoughts, ideas, people, activities, and places.

You will prevail. You were here first.

COVID 2:

A PERFECT OPPORTUNITY

Due to the unprecedented event of Coronavirus, many people have been forced to stay at home. There have been many responses to that. Some have said it is driving them up the wall (especially if they have children!) and others have said boredom has set in fast. There are also others who actually lead very solitary lives and hardly go out, such that self-isolation is merely a new way of describing their unchanged lives. What is your response?

{ LEARN TO FORGIVE YOURSELF. }

This event would have impacted your life in either a minute or massive way. It could have caused 'minor adjustment' or 'major disruption'. It would have forced you out of your normal pattern and pushed into unfamiliar situations such that your normal habits and daily actions are challenged.

Minus all the negative aspects of this unfortunate situation, I believe a perfect opportunity has arisen. This is an opportunity that many have possibly craved for but could not realise it due to 'normal living'. That is finding time for yourself.

This is a perfect opportunity to set aside time and learn more about yourself. All knowledge leads to

Self-knowledge. Many times, you do not allow yourself the time to listen to your voice within you, acknowledge your inner wisdom, and understand your deepest fears. When you hear the voice within yourself, you can truly know what you want from life and you. When you respectfully acknowledge your inner wisdom, you can find answers and inspirations that have eluded you for so long. When you honestly understand your fears, you can start to conquer them and live your life fully.

You may be terrified and loathe spending time on your own for two reasons.

Firstly, you do not really like yourself. You may have low self-esteem and the inner conversation you have with yourself is far from healthy. You prefer to get distracted by being with others, caring for others, and focusing on others so you can avoid yourself. There really is no need. You were born perfect and beautiful, exactly how you should be. Self-discovery is just that. Adults are deteriorated children. It is more of reminding yourself how beautiful you were before you acquired all the negative emotions along the journey you call 'life'. It will take time and patience. It is like when you have a new dog, you think he is going to behave in one way, but he does his own thing. It is only through time you discover that he is perfect, behaving in a way that is perfectly him.

Be patient with yourself, be generous with yourself, and, most importantly, learn to forgive yourself. You may find that falling in love with yourself may be the most rewarding and gratifying relationship ever. It is not narcissistic love. It is achieving profound self-respect, self-worth, and self-love. It is of utmost importance because the longest relationship you will ever have with anyone in your life is yourself. Make it an amazing one!

Secondly, you may want to but not know how. This is slightly easier to resolve for knowledge is in abundance through books and Google, etc. A simple way to start would be to keep a journal. Writing down your thoughts, your dreams, your fears, your daily wins or losses is a great way to acknowledge yourself. When you write, you involve approximately 40,000 nerve cells to enable that action of transferring a thought, stimulating nerves and muscles to hold a foreign object to create marks on a surface that are called 'words'. By realising a formless abstract thought into a physical form does wonders for your mind. It lets your mind know and feel that it is being listened to. You seek to be understood and the first step is listening. Persist with it for at least 66 days to see the difference. This may open your mind and lead to other ways for self-discovery.

Grab this opportunity and allow it to work for you. You ROCK and you know it!

WISDOM

Last week, I saw a dog that was brought in by a father and his son. This dog started showing aggression and has bit his guardian and his eight-year-old son a couple of times. There was talk about rehoming a vicious dog. In the consult room, the dog appeared to be very friendly and curious, just like a 14-month-old dog would. I asked the father to describe the situation leading to signs of aggression. The father replied that the dog was lying in bed and had just woken up. His son then reached over to pat the dog. That was when the dog growled and snapped. In addition, the dog had a vomiting episode the day before and diarrhoea for the past five days. The second time it bit happened under a similar situation. Prior to those incidents, it had never happened before.

> THE INTERNET HAS MADE KNOWLEDGE ABUNDANT BUT WISDOM REMAINS SCARCE.

I asked the father how he felt about the situation and he expressed his concern regarding the dog starting a path to become an aggressive dog. He was worried and concerned about the safety of his child and that it was not what he expected from a family pet. I asked the son the same question and he replied, "Next time, I will wait until he (the dog) comes to me." He said he loved the dog and did not fear him at all.

Without complicating matters and reading into it too much, it is clear that the act of aggression may have been a result of illness and circumstances created by the father and son. Once explained, the father was much relieved and professed that he loved the dog greatly and did not want to consider rehoming anyway.

What was interesting was that the son showed much more thought, consideration, empathy, and common sense in this instance. Without too much prompting or suggestion from anyone, he came up with the reason and solution himself. Wisdom certainly knows no bounds and is not restricted by age. In fact, increasing age could have negative effects on wisdom! Why is this?

When you get older, your responsibilities increase, leading to increasing fears. The fear of a child getting bitten under your care. You hear horror stories of children being mauled by certain breeds of dogs. You are exposed to horrible news in the world. The internet has brought isolated incidents of tragedy across the globe to your hands via your mobile device and into your mind.

As a 'responsible' adult, you start to make rules to bubble-wrap your children. In some primary schools, throwing snowballs is prohibited in case there is grit or soil in the snow, causing harm on impact. They are not allowed to take birthday cakes to class in case there is someone with an allergy and have a 'birthday cushion' to sit on to mark the special day instead.

The reality is, most of the time, everything will be fine. Perhaps a tiny percentage of children may get hurt by a flying snowball (whether there is grit in it or not!) and a child may not be allowed cake due to allergies (which the parent would have declared from the start of school anyway). When the children are asked about the situation, their answer is usually 'I don't mind.' It is mad to manage a risk by a widespread ban. But hey, as responsible adults, it is the right thing to do.

Sometimes, you may find answers and explanations to difficult questions through a child's eyes. You can either look for the inner child within us or simply ask a child. Let's remember that wisdom does not necessarily come with age and you were perhaps wiser in the past before your environment changed you.

The internet has made knowledge abundant, but wisdom remains scarce.

Question: Is it really true that when you get older, you get wiser?

Action Tip: Try asking a child for an answer to a problem that is baffling you.

"Wisdom doesn't necessarily come with age. Sometimes age just shows up all by itself."

– Tom Wilson

EXERCISING YOUR 651ST MUSCLE

Your muscles join certain parts of your bones to other bones and, when flexed, it enables a specific motion that allows a desired movement to occur, performing useful function. For example, your biceps (together with other muscles) when flexed allows you to scratch your head. When you contract your orbicularis oculi (eyelid muscle), you close your eyes. If you want to build your strength, you train and repeatedly flex those muscles that you want to be stronger. For example, a tennis player who desires to improve her forward serve would continuously build those relevant muscles that allow her to do so. Over time, her forward serve would be (seemingly) effortless as those muscles are now trained, used to the motion, and are strong.

> THINKING IS THE HIGHEST FUNCTION WHICH A HUMAN IS CAPABLE OF.

I remember when I had to rest my left leg after an operation for eight weeks, my calf and thigh muscles shrunk due to disuse. At that age, I have never seen or understood anything so profound before. It did not matter I had been using those muscles for 16 years before resting them for merely eight weeks, they simply went. I learnt that to keep a muscle going, you cannot just merely train it once, you have to continuously use it.

There are 650 named muscles in your body, some you actively and consciously train (going to the gym doing reps), others not so much (like your masticatory muscles that allow you to eat!). Let's discuss the 651st muscle, your brain. Ok, technically, your brain is not a muscle, but similarities exist.

Your brain is a very complex structure. It receives information from all parts of your body yet itself is not governed by a higher organ. It can sense and process pain from the body yet incapable of sensing pain itself. If you look at it, it does not appear to have any form of structure at all, just a solid mass of white-greyish matter. However, just like a muscle, it needs to be exercised. It is a powerful organ accounting for 20% of blood being pumped into it despite being only 2% of the body weight. You are borne with an enormous brain in comparison to any other animals in the world, resulting in the difficult childbirth experienced by your mother. Having a large brain can be a blessing or a curse depending on how it is used.

If not used properly, the effects can be as benign as not fulfilling your full potential or as malignant as causing mental health. You have experienced times when you feel the world is raging against you and, over time, you find that it is only you raging against yourself.

Remember that like any muscle, you need and should be exercising your brain, or more specifically, your mind constructively. If left unchecked, it can have detrimental effects as it possesses a negative bias. Thinking is the highest function which a human is capable of. Yet, unfortunately, very few people 'think'. They merely trick themselves into believing that because some mental activity is taking place in their mind, they are 'thinking'. But the truth is, most people are simply exercising the mental faculty called 'memory'. They are playing old movies, so old pictures and stories just keep flashing back on the screen of their mind.

Just like a body builder approaches in a specific way to train his muscle, you have to do the same with your brain. You need to exercise your brain wisely, deliberately, and constructively. Not only would it improve your consciousness and self-awareness, studies have shown that it can reduce certain conditions like senile dementia and Alzheimer's disease. In addition, it may also allow you to achieve your goals and make your dreams come true. It really is that powerful. So powerful that it can make or break you.

Here are a few suggestions to exercise your mind.

1. Never leave a thought incomplete.
2. Make decisions as often and as quick as you can. It allows you to see the result and learn faster (if the consequences are not desirable) for the future.
3. Write all thoughts down at the end of the day on a piece of paper (mind-dump) so you can empty your mind and rest it. You can recollect all your thoughts the next day. A clear mind will do wonders compared to a cluttered one.

Question: Can you find out exactly what stops you from thinking clearly?

Action Tip: See your mind like a room. Be aware of how you use the space inside. If you cram in too much, something is bound to fall out or get crushed.

"You can't become who you want to be because you are too attached to who you have been."

GIVING YOURSELF PERMISSION

Last week, during a seminar, an attendee asked, "I am thinking of changing vets but what is the etiquette involved in doing so?" Her concern was the complexity involved in changing vets and, if she did, would she step on toes and be blacklisted from local vets or something to that effect.

It is bewildering how pet guardians would consider changing vets to be complicated. Some are concerned that the medical history will not be passed. Some think that once you have registered your pet with a vet, it is permanent. Others have thought it to be a complicated process. A few were even concerned that they did not have the choice to change vets.

> YOUR MENTAL MODELS ARE NOT SO MUCH VIEWS AND BELIEFS THAT YOU HOLD TIGHTLY AS THEY ARE VIEWS AND BELIEFS THAT TIGHTLY HOLD YOU.

The answer could not have been further from the truth. It is extremely easy to change your vets. It is so simple that you need not even do anything but just register with the new vet of your choice. It really is that easy. Your new vets would request your pet's clinical history from your current vets and that is as complicated as it gets (not at all!).

So, why might some pet guardians feel it is complicated to start off with? Maybe it could be that, in the current society, there is a lot of fear-based systems that may have conditioned you to live 'safely', not rock the boat or make seemingly 'large' changes. For example, traffic lights indicate to you when to cross the road and when to wait. It is always interesting to watch someone waiting for the lights to turn green before crossing the road at 2 a.m. in the morning when there clearly have been no cars driving for the past hour.

More than ever, you have to learn how to give yourself permission to try new things. To allow your thoughts to be stimulated by nature and your surroundings. You should not be fearful of asking questions, trying new activities, shifting to a different routine, and challenging yourself to think different.

There was a time in your life when you thought all was possible. When you were a child, you allowed your imagination to run wild, transforming a box into a car and multiple boxes into a castle. You played make believe and if adults told you something cannot be done, you would certainly find a way to prove that it could. As you grew older, society gave you rules to follow, your teachers taught you structure, and your sense of wonder grew less and less. You start to develop beliefs and thoughts that govern the way you perceive events and how the world works.

Sometimes, you have to remind yourself of your inner child. That is so important. Your mental models are not so much views and beliefs that you hold tightly as they are views and beliefs that tightly hold you. You need to give yourself permission to be great, to be the best version of you.

Live your life with no fear. Imagine what you would accomplish ...

Question: What would you like to achieve if you found out you had only six months to live?

Action Tip: Allow yourself to believe that what you think you can't do, may be perfectly doable.

"Free your mind and the rest will follow."

– En Vogue

WHO AM I?

When someone asks you to tell them about yourself, what would you say? Would you state your job? Would you relate your hobbies, likes, and dislikes? Would you tell them your nationality? Or perhaps you are a parent?

As I grow older, my answer is no longer as simple as it was before. Would I say that I am a vet? Is that what defines me, the thing I do? Or perhaps that I am husband and a father?

The reality is, just like you, I am many things. To my clients, I am their vet. To my sons, I am their father. To my wife, I am her husband. To my parents, I am their child. To my team, I am their boss. I am different things to different people.

> **LET THE FEELINGS THAT ARE NOT SERVING YOU GO.**

Just like a multi-facet diamond, you have many faces and versions of yourself. The way you act and feel with your father is different from how it is with your mother. And it is also different when they are both present. The way you act and feel to other children is different from the way it is with your own. All those interactions and how you behave are as unique as the relationships that have been developed. They are all different and yet all exhibited by the same person: you.

As time passes, the number of facets changes. It may increase or it may decrease. One thing stays true. That is, you change with every different interaction you have with different people and it also changes collectively. For example, your interaction with A is different from B and also different when interacting with both A and B at the same time.

An interesting question would be, "How well do you know yourself?"

Many people may think that they know themselves very well. After all, you have been told that your life is a journey and of self-discovery. So many people like to think that they have gone through a journey and have 'discovered' themselves, knowing their likes, dislikes, beliefs, expectations, dreams while living life the best way they can. It is not unusual to hear someone say, "I know myself very well", "I am good at art", "I am rubbish at basketball", "That is not my type", and so on and so forth.

Now, challenge yourself with this thought …

"You are not your thoughts."

If you realise and accept that all your present thoughts and current beliefs are an accumulation of your past experiences, understanding, and interactions with the world, both environment and people, and that the future is still unknown to you and how it would possibly shape, affect, and change you, you will realise that you are perpetually changing. If you feel you know yourself, you are actually limiting yourself. If you truly believe that your interests, preferences, and skills are fixed, you are not allowing yourself to change to become more. You may know your 'past self' well but not your 'future self' for it has not happened yet.

Once you let go of the thought that 'you know yourself well' and allow further exploration, possibly trying things that you previously thought you were not good at or had no interest in, you may surprise yourself!

It is not referring to never 'knowing yourself' and understanding your strengths and weaknesses. It is just not being fixed of what you think you know about yourself and, in doing so, you are able to try more new things and grow.

In addition, you are not your feelings either. It is easy to feel down, despondent, and depressed at times and mistaking that for who or what you are. Realise that those feelings are not original, they are merely your responses and those same thoughts have been around and felt by others for eons before you, are shared by many currently, and will be experienced in the future too. Do not claim those feelings as yours and make that you. Remember the times when you felt happy and grateful. Just like those, all feelings are fleeting and not permanent, unless you give it attention and energy to retain it. Let the feelings that are not serving you go.

So, when someone asks you, "Who are you?", make your answer be "I am (Your Name) who is always striving to become the better version of myself."

Question: What do you think is your biggest weakness? Do your friends feel the same way?

Action Tip: Think of how your biggest weakness can be your advantage.

"Remind yourself: you are not your thoughts or feelings."

– Arianna Huffington

GROW LIKE BAMBOO

In a previous job, there was a vet nurse who was a year qualified and struggled with restraining cats for blood sampling. She said, "I have trained for so long and been qualified for a year and yet I am not able to do this. I must be really bad at this and maybe this is not for me at all."

This incident reminded me of a story.

There was once a man who felt discouraged. He took stock of the resolutions he made last year. Nothing in his life had changed. He was still the same person with the same problems. He began to lose hope. So, he went to speak to his mentor.

His mentor asked, "Do you know how long it takes for the giant bamboo to grow as tall as a building?"

> GROWTH TAKES PATIENCE AND PERSEVERANCE.

"During the first year, the tiny plant is watered and fertilized ... and nothing happens. It is watered and fertilized for another whole year ... and another ... and another ... and another ... and still nothing happens. Then on the fifth year, it shoots up to the sky. In six weeks, the bamboo grows 90 feet. So how long does it take for it to grow so high?"

"Six weeks," the man replied.

"That's your mistake," said the mentor. "It takes five

years. If the farmer had stopped watering the plant at any point during those five years, it would have died. What was happening in those five years was underneath the ground, an enormous network of roots was developing to support the bamboo's sudden growth. Growth takes patience and perseverance. Every drop of water makes a difference. Every step you take makes an impact. You may not see the change right away, but growth is happening."

Coming back to the vet nurse, she did not give up and persisted on her trade, learning cat by cat, restraint by restraint, clocking up the moments she did well, learning from the times she could improve, she did not give up nor did she give in. She had developed to be one of the best cat handlers and continues to give back by teaching others how to handle cats (gently of course!).

It is like going to the gym. The first day you sign on, after lifting the weights and sweating it out, if you look in the mirror, you will not see a difference. After the second session at the gym, it will still not change. You may think that it has been a complete waste of time as nothing has changed. Some give up then. That is a mistake. If you were to persist for years, the change would be evident.

Sometimes you expect too many results in too short a period of time when you are trying to change or improve something. When you do not see the results, it can be so easy to think that you are not making a difference at all. You have to learn to look past that. Not seek for instant gratification but rather, relish on delayed gratification.

I remember teaching my sons Mandarin from birth. For those who know me, will know that I blatantly refuse to speak to my sons in English but only converse in Mandarin. I felt that English was a given living in the United Kingdom and wanted to preserve their Chinese heritage by teaching them Mandarin. It was not easy. Speaking a language no one else is using to a new-born baby, six months old, one year old, I really had no idea how much was going in and how much impact I was making. They would look back, smile a bit, gurgle a bit, mutter something, and crawl away. I really had no idea. Then suddenly, they started to reply in Mandarin, singing in Mandarin, and even reciting Chinese proverbs! It was unexpected and it was beautiful. I understood that all the time when I was speaking Mandarin to them, and seemingly had no response, their little minds were quietly processing the sounds, the meaning, and slowly (but surely) training their tongues to finally utter those first words in Chinese when they were ready. It was amazing. I just needed to be patient.

Consider the skill you want to learn, the dream you want to fulfil, and the goal you want to reach. What are you doing today that is going to take you closer to that skill, dream, or goal? What are you willing to do to make your dreams come true? Are you willing to do whatever it takes? Are you willing to take action even if all the odds are stacked against you? Are you willing to push past your fears and doubts, including all around who would give you 'good advice' and tell you to quit? How much faith and belief are you willing to have?

Like a well-built skyscraper, you need to lay the foundations down slowly but surely for success to come. Patience and perseverance are key.

Question: Is there any particular reason that makes you think success should be fast? Is it being reflected in your surroundings?

Action Tip: Speak to people who have succeeded, especially those who achieved 'over-night' success, and ask them how long it took them and what they did to get there.

"Most people overestimate what they can achieve in one year and underestimate what they can achieve in ten years."

– Bill Gates

KNOWLEDGE IS NOT POWER

The three most dangerous words when it comes to learning are, "I know that". Once those words have been uttered, mentally, the mind stops any input of information and, physically, it may stop the person volunteering the information to continue giving.

UNTIL KNOWLEDGE IS APPLIED IN SOME FORM, IT DOES NOT CHANGE ANYTHING.

It has been said that to be an expert in anything, one needs to have done at least 10,000 hours of that skill set or art. For example, the requirement for a pilot before being allowed to fly a commercial flight would require at least 10,000 hours of simulated flight time. Does that mean that there is no more learning that needs to be done after that? Is it true that one can know so much that there is nothing else to learn? Many masters, experts, leaders, and teachers would agree that to be and remain the best in their field, they have to become the humblest students. The more you learn about a certain subject, the more you realise there is more to learn. No one can know so much that there is nothing left to learn, and no one can know so little that there is nothing they can teach. So how much is there actually to learn?

Let's pretend you are sitting in a room. Using that as a metaphor for knowledge, where you are sitting right now is what you know you know. Around the room is what you know you do not know, for example, if there was a cupboard, you know there is something in the cupboard though you do not know what it is. However, you are aware you do not know that. Outside the room lies what you do not know you do not know. That is where you are not even aware of what you are ignorant of. The world is a huge place with infinite things to learn. One's journey to knowledge is a never-ending one.

After learning something, it still does not mean you have done or changed anything. Knowledge is not power. Applied knowledge is power. Many people can read a lot and learn a lot. However, they do not take any action to apply it, they merely know it. Until knowledge is applied in some form, it does not change anything. Knowledge not applied will only remain to be merely thoughts until action is taken using those same thoughts to affect any changes. And there lies the difference. Have you ever observed a situation where the same knowledge is imparted to two individuals and they both get different results? Or two persons looking at the same painting or listening to the same piece of music and having totally different interpretations?

So, the opportunity for knowledge provision can be given but a unique factor that is involved in the outcome lies with what you do with that knowledge. You can choose not to take any action, resulting in no change in outcome. Or a choice can be made to apply the knowledge and some action will be taken, resulting in some different results. In addition, the result will depend on how you interpreted and applied the knowledge. Until you apply the knowledge, it does not make a difference and hence is not power.

When you learn something that you believe in and agree with, it is important that you do not just allow it to remain as thoughts in your mind. You should strive to apply that knowledge however suitable. You have to understand that knowing something is not enough and will not change anything. It is only when you apply the knowledge that you can have the power to make a difference.

Question: What knowledge do you possess currently that you can apply to give you results that you desire? What is holding you back?

Action Tip: Just do it. If you get it right, great. If not, you learn. Either way, you will receive result.

"It is not enough to know what to do, you also need to do what you know."

– Tony Robbins

EMPTY YOUR CUP

Having a Chinese heritage, one of my favourite Kung Fu actors is Bruce Lee. Bruce was not only a great martial artist and actor; he was also a great philosopher. Considering he was only around for a little over three decades (he died when he was 33 years old), he made a huge impact around the world.

Here is one of his stories. Back in 1964, Joe Hyams met with the legendary man for the very first time to see if Bruce would teach him privately. This is Joe's account of the encounter.

"Why do you want to study with me?" Bruce asked.

"Because I was impressed with your demonstration and because I've heard you are the best."

"You've studied other martial arts?" he asked.

> UNTIL YOU LIVE IT, YOU DO NOT KNOW IT.

"For a long time," I answered, "but I stopped some time ago and now I want to start over again."

"Do you realize you will have to unlearn all you have learned and start over again?" he asked.

"No," I said.

Bruce smiled and placed his hand lightly on my shoulder. "Let me tell you a story my master told me," he said. "It is about the Japanese Zen master who received a university professor who came to inquire about Zen. It was obvious to the master from the start of the conversation that the professor was not so much interested in learning about Zen as he was in impressing the master with his own opinions and knowledge. The master listened patiently and finally suggested they have tea. The master poured his visitor's cup full and then kept on pouring. The professor watched the cup overflowing until he could no longer restrain himself. 'The cup is overfilled; no more will go in.' 'Like the cup,' the master said, 'you are full of your own opinions and speculations. How can I show you Zen unless you first empty your cup?'"

Bruce studied my face. "You understand the point?"

"Yes," I said. "You want me to empty my mind of past knowledge and old habits so that I will be open to new learning."

"Precisely," said Bruce. "And now we are ready to begin your first lesson."

Many times you bring a lot of 'baggage' with you when you want to learn something. You carry beliefs, expectations, perspectives, opinions, and pre-conceived ideas when learning. How are you meant to learn when you already know so much? The three most dangerous words one could ever utter when learning are, 'I know that'. Once those words are said, very little information is able to penetrate into the mind for the mind is already full and closed.

There are various reasons why you may do that. Sometimes, you do not want to appear stupid. Maybe it is because you feel you are expected to know that. Maybe you are too shy to admit your ignorance. Maybe you are not interested in learning more. Maybe you really think you know it all. Until you live it, you do not know it.

Knowledge is truly boundless. Einstein said, "Two things are infinite, the Universe and human stupidity, and I am not yet completely sure about the universe." You simply do not know everything. To think that you do is just plain arrogant, silly, and more importantly, inaccurate.

In the pet industry, there are so many opinions out there. Is feeding dogs raw food dangerous? Is it the best food? Is neutering your pet necessary? Are we able to make cats 'indoor' only? Does acupuncture work? Do animals feel pain? Is homeopathy effective? Are vaccinations completely safe and compulsory? Are pets an entitlement or a luxury? And many more questions that have so many 'answers' or merely opinions.

If you truly want to learn, you need to empty your cup. No matter how full, it is a prerequisite for learning. The usefulness of a cup is its emptiness. To better improve your skills as pet guardians, you need to empty your cups to learn. Education is a two-way thing. The most effective masters are also the most diligent students. The more you learn about anything, the more you will realise you know nothing.

In my work, I find consultations most fulfilling when you taught me something about you or your pet that I did not know before. I also find that treatment plans are most effective when I am working with you to walk me through both you and your pet's habits. It is a collaboration between you and I to come up with the treatment plan, not just me telling you what to do.

> **Question**: Are you able to completely clear your mind when learning something new? If not, what holds you back?
>
> **Action Tip**: Remember you get the most insight when you have no preconceived ideas.

"A cup is only useful when empty."

– Bruce Lee

THE POWER OF COMPOUND KNOWLEDGE

If you were offered a choice of £1 million pounds as a one off or £0.01 that doubles daily for a month (31 days), which one would you choose?

Most people would choose a million pounds for it is an obviously massive amount and available immediately. Einstein has said that compound interest is the eighth wonder of the world. That is why banks and mortgage lenders exist and that is how they make money, by compound interest. Same for property owners, both accruing rent and property value increasing over time.

Day	£	Day	£	Day	£	Day	£
1	0.01	8	1.28	15	164	22	20,971.52
2	0.02	9	2.56	16	327.68	23	41,943.04
3	0.04	10	5.12	17	655.36	24	83,886.08
4	0.08	11	10.2	18	1,310.72	25	167,772.16
5	0.16	12	20.5	19	2,621.44	26	335,544.32
6	0.32	13	41	20	5,242.88	27	671,088.64
7	0.64	14	81.9	21	10,485.76	28	1,342,177.28

Day	£
29	2,684,354.56
30	5,368,709.12
31	10,737,418.24

If you take a look at the picture in this article, you will find that after 31 days of doubling one penny, the end product is more than £10 million pounds, 10 times more than the first offer of a million pounds. There lies the power of compound interest.

Now, challenge yourself with the idea of compound knowledge. When learning a new skill, entering a new job, or learning a language, the initial stages are devastatingly hard. To introduce a new concept and willing your mind to pick up new thoughts, new ideas, or a new mind-set, it

> IF ONLY YOU HAD PERSISTED TILL THE END.

can be painfully alien and difficult. Even if it seems that you have been doing it and practicing it for a long time, it can still feel as though nothing has changed and nothing has improved.

Looking at the picture again, at Day 7 (£0.64), Day 14 (£81.90) and even Day 21 (almost £10,500), the amounts seemed like nothing compared to the instant gratification of one million pounds in the alternative offer. So, if you were to use a month (31 days) to compare with the journey of mastering a skill, a job, or a language, even at three quarters of the way, you may still feel you have not learnt anything at all and, god forbid, you may give up then, thinking that it was not meant to be, that you were not meant to excel at whatever you were learning.

That would be a grave mistake, for if you had persisted on, you would have seen the fruits of your labour at the last stretch of the journey. It is only at Day 30 and 31 where you would see how far you had come, what you have learnt, and how much you know now compared to when you started. If only you had persisted till the end.

Sometimes it is easy to despair and give up, especially when you are not seeing the results you were expecting. Do not give up. Never give up. Look at adversity in the eye and know that by persisting, you will gain the outcome of compound knowledge. You need to show grit, resilience, and fortitude in achieving your goals and dreams.

Question: Are you able to repeatedly, without question, improve in tiny amounts on your passion?

Action Tip: Understand that success is made up of tiny wins made consistently over a long period of time.

"At some point it comes down to who can handle the boredom of training every day, doing the same lifts over and over. The greatest threat to success is not failure but boredom."

– James Clear

LESSONS FROM A BABY

A new-born baby is fairly helpless, lying on her back. Through her eyes, she sees beings bigger than her walking around on two legs. She does not know how she is going to do it, but she sees the possibility of the action. She absorbs in her mind through her senses, mainly vision. When she gets older, she tries to move.

First, she wriggles her legs and put her hands up in the air. Slowly, she rolls and learns that she can move around by rolling but it is not enough. She turns over on her front and finds that she can move her hands and legs to crawl! One step further to increasing the speed she moves. But it is hardly enough. She has seen what others can do. She grabs the side of a chair and tries to stand. Over time, she manages to let go and actually stands on her own! Result!

FAIL FAST, FAIL OFTEN, FAIL BIG AND FAIL FORWARD.

This is where the miracle truly begins … Through NO teaching, NO instructions, NO lessons, she begins to attempt walking. She takes her first half step; she stumbles and sits on her bottom. She tries again and falls again. She tries and fails again. This happens repeatedly. She does not give up. She does not give in. She continues to try every day and every time she gets a chance. Finally, she walks and eventually runs, hops, and skips!

A child, without being taught, knows the importance of not giving up. There are no courses on walking for a baby. How does a baby learn to walk? First, seeing the possibility of success by observing those performing it. Second, by trying and trying and trying again and not giving up. The idea of giving up is alien to her. Finally, she succeeds using her simple but effective Two-Steps-to-Success Method.

How many times do you give up in life just because you failed at the first or subsequent attempts? You would not dream of telling a child to give up walking after she has fallen for the hundredth time and say that, "You are not meant for walking. This is the best you can be." But if you fail at something, you feel disappointed and, perhaps, you try again. Over time, you may give up. What has happened to the innate miraculous gift you had when you were born and how you never give up, no matter what, resulting in pretty much a 100% success rate as you are actually walking without being taught?! How did you lose that gift when you grew older and (supposedly) smarter? Where did the fear from failing come from?

There are lessons to be learnt from children. Fail fast, fail often, fail BIG, and fail forward. Did Thomas Edison give up after trying hundreds of materials for the filament of the light bulb? There is an innate power within you. Look inside, remember your inner child, and maximise your life.

Question: Can you recall the time you felt you were invincible? Can you remember how you felt?

Action Tip: Develop an appetite for failure, knowing it brings you closer to success.

"Success is the ability to go from failure to failure without any loss of enthusiasm."

– Winston Churchill

BEING IN THE FLOW –

LEARNING FROM ANIMALS

One of the hardest skills to learn and master when working with animals is animal handling. This is not referring to cuddling animals, playing with them, or carrying them around (though that takes a certain skill and technique in some cases!). It is about positioning them to allow minor procedures to be done in the veterinary context. For example, holding a dog's or cat's legs or neck exposed for blood sampling or drug administration, holding their claws for clipping, keeping the head still for an intricate eye examination or simply keeping cats on the table, while the otoscope is being placed in her/his ears.

> YOU AMPLIFY EMOTIONS AND THOUGHTS.

Notice the word 'restraint' has not been used. There are different methods to achieve the above tasks. Some of them are holding the animal very firmly, almost like a restraint. This may be controversial to some. In my experience, restraint is only useful or necessary in the smallest of situations. The majority of the situations, working with the animal to facilitate what needs to be done is preferred. It is like applying a hold that allows the animal to stay in a comfortable position with minimal strength. By staying in that position, the animal is kept comfortable to allow the procedure to be performed. It is not easy.

Some people do it naturally where others struggle. It involves understanding the anatomy very well, so you know where to place your fingers, arms, body to make sure the animal feels in contact and held in isolation at the same time. It also requires the understanding of each individual's temperament and mood at that moment in time. Fundamentally, it is acknowledging that those essential procedures that are performed are unnatural for the animal and it is not able to understand why it is being done. It should be approached with finesse, empathy, patience, and understanding that the pet have no clue to what is being done without its consent.

Working with animals can allow you to understand about BEING IN THE FLOW. They are natural beings that react on instinct and respond to their environment. You are more complicated as you are built with higher faculties. You amplify emotions and thoughts. When you work with an animal, you have to understand the flow of them to be able to actually work with them and not just force them to do something that you think needs to be done. In doing so, it will allow you to understand nature and yourself better.

It will allow you to understand life better as well. Looking for what is natural for you, appreciating little sense of ease here and there and enjoying BEING IN THE FLOW whenever you can. It can be such a powerful feeling that allows increased productivity, greater self-understanding/appreciation and learning about your power within and what you are capable of.

Be sure to explore, find the FLOW, and experience it first-hand for it is amazing …

> **Question**: Have you ever experienced your 'flow' state? Are you able to recreate it whenever you desire?
>
> **Action Tip**: Learn breathing exercises and practice mindfulness.

"Water is what it is, and does what it does. It can overwhelm but it's not overwhelmed. It can be still, but it is not impatient. It can be forced to change course, but it is not frustrated."

Challenge

HAVING A LITTLE FAITH

Sarah had spent almost eight months training her 18-month-old male German Shorthaired Pointer, Toby, in recall. Toby had a knack for wandering off and 'exploring the world'. He would love to smell the roses, take his time, and when he picks up a scent, he dashes off like an arrow in pursuit. When that happens, Sarah finds that recalling him back is like trying to stop the tide from rising up the shore, an impossible task apart from divine intervention. As such, Sarah had invested in multiple training courses and spent countless hours practicing, more spent in running, shouting and whistling, and waving bits of cheesy treats (which Toby loves) after a hound that never wants to come back.

> YOU SEE WHAT YOU WANT TO SEE. YOU PROCESS WHAT YOUR MIND WANTS TO PROCESS. YOU HEAR WHAT YOU WANT TO HEAR.

One day, Sarah was out walking with Toby, off the lead, of course. While she was pondering in her thoughts about life and such, her mobile rang. The news was not good. Her aging mother had fallen down and only barely managed to call her for help. She sounded frightened and was panicking due to the pain she felt in her hips. She needed Sarah immediately. Sarah calmly assured her the best she could and ended the call. She then frantically looked up to search for Toby. "Man, that dog! Where are you?!" she thought, "We have got to go!"

She saw him about 40m away, standing erect and sniffing the air. He had caught a scent. Sarah willed all her inner belief, mustered all her calmness, and began to call him back. "I need you back here now, Toby! Please help. Please listen. Don't go chasing that scent! We have not got the time!" She recognized that look, the look that mixed determination and adventure. He had caught a scent and would not let it go. His head was up, and tail pointed back straight as an arrow. A few more seconds and he would be gone like the wind. Something broke his chain of thought, Toby looked back at Sarah. He saw her face and hands waving for him to come back. He looked at the direction of the scent. To Sarah's disbelief, he abandoned the scent and began to run back to Sarah. Somehow, he must have felt Sarah's need and urgency. Sarah and Toby then raced off to aid her mum in need.

In life, sometimes you are faced with situations that you may feel you know the inevitable outcome. You have seen it before. You have experienced it before. Perhaps it is someone you know that will react in a certain way. When I was fifteen, money was extremely tight at home. My mum gave me $50 as spending money for the weekend. Unfortunately, I lost the money carelessly on the bus trip. It must have fallen out unnoticed. I was horrified and felt so bad. I felt worse about it as I knew what my mum was going to say when I told her. I knew that I would be chastised like before and be reminded how 'money does not grow on trees and we must be more careful'. I could not enjoy the day at all as I felt bad the whole time, anticipating the carnage I was about to face.

When I got home, I told my mum what happened and waited for the explosion (my mum had quite the fiery temper in her days!). She looked at me and quietly said, "How do you feel?" I replied that I was sorry and felt really bad. All she said, in an even but caring voice, was, "It happens. Sometimes we lose things. Be more careful in the future." There was no explosion, no emotions flying, and certainly no carnage! I have never felt more relieved. That day I learned an important lesson. Well, quite a few, actually. The obvious one was that I had to be more careful about storing money safely (that did not stop me from losing more money in the future by carelessness! We can do but try!) and learning that allowing unfounded fears to ruin my day was a bit pointless. More importantly, I learned that having a little faith goes a long way.

Sometimes people, situations, and events may surprise you. If you have lost the faith, even when good things happen unexpectedly, you would not see them and merely revert to 'auto-pilot' in your view of the world. You see the world through your filters. You see what you want to see. You process what your mind wants to process. You hear what you want to hear. If you do not have faith that people (and life) are inherently good and adopt a negative view, life will be incredibly tough. You will face a series of self-fulfilling prophecies that your life is hard, and nothing comes easy. Any good luck, a positive twist of fate, or incredible fortune will be viewed as anomalies and disregarded. You will find life hard because life is hard in your view. You will become like the amazing Charlie Brown.

However, if you have a little faith (and keep the faith), you will live in a life of positive expectancy. This is not referring to wishful thinking or living life carelessly just because you believe everything will be fine and good, for that is truly a recipe for disaster! It is living your life the best you could and still believe that something good, something great, can happen to and for you anytime. To have that constant positive expectancy so when a perfect twist of fate occurs, you are ready to embrace it, practice your ever-increasing gratitude for it, and relish in your unexpected great fortune. Keeping the faith is so important. Be aware that you see the world through filters. Be sure to put 'Positive Expectancy' as one of your filters!

Perhaps, in time to come, the Toby in your life will surprise you. Be sure you are ready to receive the shock (and pleasure)!

Question: When was the last time something unexpectedly good happened to you?

Action Tip: Keep your mind open. Remember that you will seek what your mind is prepared to receive.

"Lord we gotta keep the faith."

– Jon Bon Jovi

WINTER IS COMING

Your life has seasons. Spring for fresh starts, Summer for greatness, and Autumn for reaping rewards. These seasons have a great purpose in your life. What about winter? Winter is when things go wrong, broken relationships, lost jobs, failed investments, illness, or even death may occur. It is when the stark coldness strikes your heart and soul with despair, fear, and exasperation. It is the time when you cry out, "Why me?", "Give me a break!" and "I can't take this anymore, I am in too much pain!"

What is the whole point of having low moments in your life? How do you cope with your winter?

Winter is a time when you get a chance to really see yourself. It takes away all the distractions of pleasantries of life, the convenience of nature, and any hint of positivity that you may expect. It is only when you are stripped bare of your ego, success, and superficiality are you able to see with crystal-clear clarity what you are made of.

> USE YOUR EMOTIONS TO THINK BUT DON'T THINK WITH YOUR EMOTIONS.

Success is a horrible teacher. It merely reflects and rewards what you have done. It hardly teaches anything new. Nothing fails faster than success. Adversity, on the other hand, is an excellent teacher.

It categorically shows you what you have done is not deemed right by the universe. Adversity gives you an opportunity to test yourself to see how much will power your possess. It also forces you to learn many truths you would never have discovered without it.

But adversity does more than this. Adversity may open doors that you have not seen or thought of before. It can lead you to an understanding of self and your power within that was never known or released without it.

In those moments when things are going horribly wrong, where life seems to throw curveballs at you from every corner, when all you want to do is to crawl away and die, don't. Embrace your winter, just like how you would embrace your other seasons. Do not ignore or bury it. It has happened for a purpose. Allow yourself to feel it deeply and completely. Delve into it and understand it. Search for the precious lesson behind it. Use your winter to understand yourself better. The cost of adversity can only escalate if you do not find the lesson behind it. Use your emotions to think but don't think with your emotions.

Be grateful for the lesson bestowed upon you. This may be the hardest to accept, much less do. How can you be grateful when all you feel is sadness, anger, resentment, fear, and despair? Remember that you are alive. You are still in the game of life. All these feelings are part of life. You were not assured that your life would only consist of everything nice. The fact that you are having all the difficult feelings mentioned earlier shows that you are truly living. Be grateful to be allowed to feel and understand what life has to bring. You are truly living life, every aspect of it, the good, the bad, and the ugly.

So, embrace your winter. Use it to dig down to your core and have a chat with him/her. Understand him/her better and have a discussion on how to grow from this. Nurture your core. Know that by doing so, you will emerge bigger, better, and stronger. Your life will be more substantial and richer in so many ways that it cannot be achieved without your winter. Some of the biggest failures in life are people who have never failed.

Know that if you are going through Winter, Spring is just around the corner. When Winter comes, open your arms and welcome it into your life. It is truly your friend and teacher.

Question: Are you able to find opportunity in the saddest, most unlucky, disappointing, and tragic part of your life?

Action Tip: Start small. Be grateful that you have survived the experience. Then you can start to find small lessons to learn from that will lead to larger results.

"Life gives no one immunity against adversity, but life gives to everyone the power of positive thought, which is sufficient to master all circumstances of adversity and convert them into benefits."

– Napoleon Hill

DELVE DEEPER

Spot was a three-year-old rescued Jack Russell/Chihuahua cross. He was usually extremely sweet, friendly, loves cuddles and tummy rubs. He was the sort of dog who would come up to you, tail wagging, and push his muzzle on your legs as if to beckon, "Your job is to play with me now!"

However, when you started to stroke his head and ears, his attitude would change. He would begin to growl and, if you continued, he may snap. This usually

{ HURT PEOPLE
HURT PEOPLE. }

brings confusion to anyone who was interacting with him for the first time. It was revealed that his previous owner had hit him on his head repeatedly as a method of training when he did something wrong. His reaction was a result of his past experience.

In life, your behaviours and reactions are usually a manifestation and interpretation of your past experiences. When you observe a child interacting with a new emotion for the first time, it is usually of curiosity and wonder instead of wariness and caution. For example, he may approach a stinging nettle as he would a dandelion. It is only when he has been stung once, then his next interaction may be met with caution and possibly fear.

You can reflect this in your interactions with others. When you are happy with others (interacting positively), it is usually because your past experiences have shown you that the results would be positive. When you are not so nice to others, it is also usually because your past experiences have taught you that the outcome was not very pleasant.

With this in mind, it brings understanding when someone (could be family, friend, or stranger) is being horrible to you, it may not be because of you. It could be his past bad experiences that have brought about this resulting behaviour. Hurt people hurt people. That person is usually hurting inside, hence merely expressing his hurt with his interactions with the outside world. You just happen to be there.

Do you know how tiring it is to be angry, resentful, and hurtful to others? Have you experienced the energizing lightness of happiness, contentment, peace, and joy when you interact positively with another? If you were to choose, what would be your choice? Certainly, it would be more sensible, logical, and beneficial to choose the latter. Why would anyone choose to exert more energy that results in horrible feelings by being nasty to others? Perhaps, they are in pain. They are hurtful because they are hurting inside. They cause pain because they are in pain. They are angry towards you because they are angry inside (usually at themselves).

Do not take it personally. It usually has nothing to do with you. You may be a factor that escalated their feelings, but the fundamental core of the issue usually has nothing to do with you (unless you intentionally went about to cause harm which means that you were probably harmed before). When someone is not able to forgive others, usually they are not able to forgive themselves. To know all is to forgive all. When a stranger shouts at you, it probably has more to do with his past than your present actions. It is the same when it is someone you know.

Remember when someone is being nasty to you, possess the inner confidence to be able to see past the immediate reaction, find strength to delve deeper, and understand why he is reacting that way. Fortify your internal strength and know that no one can bring you down without your permission. If you possess the skills, find out what is causing the pain in that person to make him react that way. After all, it is more energizing to be pleasant than nasty. The aftertaste of both reactions will be amplified in the person who expresses them. If you are nice to others, you feel better inside. If you are horrible to a person, you feel more horrible inside.

By not reacting superficially to another's less-than-desirable behaviour, and delving deeper into the underlying reason, you would not only feel better about yourself but also possibly help the other. People crave to be understood.

By the way, Toby loves his head being rubbed now!

Question: What assumptions do you have about yourself and the person who is being hurtful to you? Are they necessarily true?

Action Tip: Accept that you may not be the (complete) reason why the other party is angry, upset, or hurt. Don't forget to breathe and smile.

"Many have no desire to understand what you say or do. They just want to be understood."

COVID 3:

CORONA, NOT THE BEER

All are undergoing strange times during this coronavirus outbreak. Apart from the chaos this virus has created, it has also caused mass panic and fear. It has affected how you live, how you think, and how you behave.

The virus is here, and the situation is real. There is not much you can do about it. How can you remain positive in these trying times? The secret is gratitude. The Attitude of Gratitude is paramount. Gratitude is feeling thankful. The habit of gratitude can greatly help the feelings of inner peace and improve self-awareness.

YOUR INTERNAL WORLD IS YOURS TO DECIDE, CREATE AND MANAGE.

It connects us to the present moment, uplifts our spirit, and feeds our heart. It is also the antidote to fear. You simply cannot feel gratitude and fear at the same time. It doesn't mean settling for less or not making every effort to take safety precautions. Quite the opposite. It is appreciating and loving what you have while dreaming of the future when you will be safe again.

You will face challenges in life from time to time. Some small, some large. You may not be able to choose what situations may bring but you can certainly choose how you think. No matter what or how you think, the external world remains unaffected. However, your internal world is yours to decide, create, and manage.

If you have forgotten to be thankful in your life, to your family, those that surround you, your achievements, your failures, and your unpursued dreams, now is the time to rectify that. Tell them, tell yourself, write them a letter, proclaim it, and announce it. You may be fearful and stressed, only if you allow it. You may lose loved ones, you may fall sick, your business may fail, and what you took for granted may be taken away from you. Be sure to take stock the things that you actually have now and be immensely grateful for them.

Your life will be changed, directly or indirectly, there is no doubt about that. Shops that you frequent often may close. Small businesses that rely on daily footfall and turnover are affected greatly. Hold your ground, don't despair.

Social distancing is healthy. Emotional distancing is not. Be mindful, be kind. Mary, an 80-year-old lady, was doing her shopping last week and she received plenty of comments from strangers about her being out and how she should have stayed at home. It is hard to think that what she can do in her life is dictated by her age. She can't stay at home indefinitely. Hold your ground, be kind.

Remember that there are still many things in the world that deserve your power, your energy, and your time. The virus has done enough damage by taking many lives around the world already. Do not give it permission to cause more harm in your internal world, your mind.

Keep the faith. Be grateful. Take care of yourself and take care of those around you. Balance living like there is no tomorrow with behaving like you'll live forever.

Wishing you all the best in health, heart, mind, and soul. Be safe.

Question: Have you got any gratitude unexpressed in your heart?

Action Tip: Write at least five things you are grateful for before going to bed daily.

YOU CAN'T BE SEEN

UNTIL YOU LEARN TO SEE

A dog guardian was struggling with her five-month-old Cockerpoo puppy. She was saying that the puppy has developed a bad habit of biting everything, from objects to people's hands (more mouthing than biting). She is at her wits end as he had chewed her card wallet with all her bank cards and also her favourite dressing gown!

A puppy chewing things is about the most natural act to do when they are teething. Their new teeth are growing and they will feel the urge to chew. It is interesting how that act should be perceived as good or bad. There is no good or bad to it, it just is. Sometimes, we judge or evaluate an action more than trying to understand why it was done. When we actually understand why the puppy was chewing, we can then empathise and realise that he was trying to tell us something, "I need to chew! I can't help it! If you don't want me to chew

> VERY RARELY DO WE PERMIT OURSELVES TO *UNDERSTAND* PRECISELY WHY A PERSON HAS SAID SOMETHING.

things I should not chew, then show me and teach me what I can chew!"

In our daily interactions with others in life, it is not dissimilar. Our first reaction to most of the statements (which we hear from other people) is an evaluation or judgement, rather than an understanding of it. Very rarely do we permit ourselves to *understand* precisely why the person had said it. We tend to react (putting our emotions into the response) and not really seek to understand. When someone says, "I think you are being unfair", our reaction would be to justify why he was wrong (if we were actually fair) or why that person was right (if we had been unfair). Very rarely do we seek to understand or ask the question, "Why did he just say that? What triggered him to have such emotions that resulted in that question being asked?" When we ask ourselves that question and seek to understand, we are truly attempting to understand the other. Our response may be vastly different.

Children often make great comments, having fewer filters than adults. I know my son, half an hour after a full lunch, would say, "I am hungry". My first reaction (like most parents, I have been told) would be of incredulity and say something along the lines of "you should be full after lunch", "wait till dinner time" or "you need to slow down and let your food digest". Putting the above concept of true understanding in play, I asked, "Interesting … why did you say that?" Of which, he promptly replied, "I saw that boy having an ice cream and suddenly remembered about our trip to the beach and buying the ice cream then. It was a great day!" We then continued to have one of the most enjoyable conversations which I know would not have happened if I had responded with my first reaction. He was not wanting more food. He was merely recalling a memory that meant a lot to him.

So, next time when your dog does something you did not expect or is undesirable, hold your actions, check your thoughts, and seek first to understand. It may change your response and emotions to a more favourable one. Likewise, in your daily interactions, the next statement that is directed at you or said to you (that requires thought and a response), ask yourself, "Why did he (or she) just say that? What made he (or she) say that?" Seek first to understand, the results may astound you.

Question: Do you find yourself answering questions in a certain way? Does it stimulate a certain response?

Action Tip: Literally wait three seconds before answering any question. Use that time to ask yourself why that person asked the question.

"You can't be seen until you learn to see."

– Seth Godin

MANIFESTATION OF FEAR

The pet guardian had mentioned that River, the three-year-old Lakeland Terrier, was nervous before the consultation so the vet was prepared. When he first saw her at the waiting area, he started barking and lunged towards her. In the consultation room, she chatted with his guardian, ignoring River. He approached her, sniffing extremely tentatively. She offered him treats which he took readily. She seemed to be making progress. His tail was wagging but still extremely cautious. When she finished treating him (six pieces in all), he waited for two seconds and decided that she was still a threat and started barking and lunging again.

> DIFFERENT PEOPLE MANIFEST FEAR DIFFERENTLY.

She knew he was not angry at her (as he barely knew her!) and yet, he displayed such aggression. It came from nervousness and fear seemingly translating into anger. How often in life do you exhibit anger and irritation that had arisen from fear?

When I was a child, I remember my mother telling me off for not letting her know where I was. At that time, I thought she was angry at me but now I realised that it was due to fear of any mishap happening to me.

When I look back at various episodes in my life where I experienced anger or when someone had been angry at me, I can almost always trace it back to the initial emotion of fear. There was the fear of losing a loved one, fear of losing one's identity, fear of losing face (being shamed), fear of losing power, fear of inadequacy, fear of failure, fear of the future, fear of the past repeating itself, fear of not being enough, and many more others.

It can be very misleading to others when the anger was displayed as they might have not understood or the ability to comprehend that the anger had arisen from fear, not because you were truly angry with them. Many conflicts have arisen from fear. Wars have been started because of fear.

Fear is truly the mind killer. Different people manifest fear differently. Some show aggression, some show withdrawal, some talk excessively, some show physical signs like biting nails, some become overfriendly, and some put on a front.

It is important to recognize these manifestations as it can help you understand that the individual is actually fearful and addressing the fear may increase the chance of a positive outcome. It is not easy to accept that the individual is not really angry at you. The circumstances and situation may be much more complicated than that. It could stem from past bad experiences, low self-esteem, and fear of various issues.

On the other hand, if you fail to understand the basis of the behaviour and purely take it at face value, you may react thinking it was personal. This may escalate the situation and increase the chance of a negative outcome. The approach is extremely similar whether it is a dog or a person showing signs of aggression due to fear.

Fear causes irrational actions. Are you able to curb your fears or at least recognize when you are fearful and be more mindful of your actions? Are you able to understand that it is not the dog's intention to attack, though it may appear that way, but it is actually showing its defence?

Question: What is your number one fear that holds you back from your great achievement?

Action Tip: Write your fears down in your journal. Fear is imaginary. Writing it down reduces its 'mysterious' power.

"Fear is the mind killer."

– Leto in 'Children of Dune'

BEING JUDGED

If you speak to pet guardians of different breed dogs, especially if they had researched deeply into the breed either before or after caring for their dogs, you will find something very interesting. Invariably, they (not all!) would say there were specific traits unique to that breed. What is interesting is those traits can be quite similar to each breed. For example, a Dalmatian guardian might say that their dog can be 'mental' which is very similar to what a Chocolate Labrador guardian would say.

{ GET OUT OF YOUR EGO AND GET INTO THEIRS! }

However, there are also calm examples of both breeds. Would you make assumptions of either breeds? It may be wiser to take each dog as they are. They are unique in their character and temperament. They are all beautiful in their own right.

Extending this observation, let's discuss you, the pet guardian. Do you feel that you are being judged at your vets? There may be clichés like 'rich' people if you drive up in a new BMW or a Land Rover, poor people if you live in council estates, 'dog' people if you are a trainer or a behaviourist, 'breeders' if you breed from your pet, and many various types.

Clichés and people are not always what they seem. There are 'rich' people incurring bad debts and seemingly poor people pulling out cash to pay their bills. There are breeders being both ethical and unethical in their dealings. There are people with 'dog' experience showing excellent understanding of their pet and pet guardianship and also those with a warped sense of what pet guardianship is. It is important to understand the background of each individual for it helps to set the stage to build on but view each one as a unique person as it is truly what they are.

To be likable (important for a vet for it does help in building trust and, ultimately, improve the clinical outcome), you have to like others for who they are. No assumptions, no clichés, no biasness. Only then you can truly treat each one as a dear and valued friend to enable the best possible working relationship.

Everyone has their own way of expressing themselves and they may not be who they seem. There was a client who always looks as though she was going to hit us on the head, but she remained to be one of our best clients who truly appreciated us and was wholly supportive. On the other hand, there were clients that seemingly showed warmth and openness only to leave without a warning. Go figure!

Those who judge others are secretly in fear of being judged by others. It usually comes with low self-esteem. By practising not to judge (like any skill, practising helps!), you can actually build your self-esteem in fearing less of being judged by others and become a better version of yourself. It is truly miraculous when you start looking at others like a child, no presumptions, no expectations held, and just enjoy discovering each other for who they are. It brings back the kindred human spirit and sense of wonder that is sometimes lacking in this world. If you take the view that everyone is inherently good and they are only acting the best they could in their present understanding, you will constantly be grateful for all interactions.

Instead of judging others, invest the energy in asking "Why". "Why did they do that?", "Why did they think like that?", "Why have they made that decision?", "What do they feel like that?" are powerful questions that would increase your learning instead of feeling negative for being judged personally. Get out of your ego and get into theirs!

Question: What is a little cue you can introduce to yourself to break your pattern from judging others?

Action Tip: Give trust before the other party deserves or 'earns' it.

"If you judge people, you have no time to love them."

– Mother Teresa

BE PREPARED

Lord Baden Powell (Founder of the Scouting Movement) said that "Scouting is a game for boys". I joined the movement at the tender age of 11. The uniform was donned and a lot of time was spent perfecting the way to roll the scarf and to place the woggle after. The pride felt during the Investiture to join the ranks of my fellow brothers was immense. The campfire nights and singing to our hearts' content was unforgettable. We sang numerous scouting songs which I still sing to my sons to this day. Various skills were taught, from building wooden structures (pioneering) to learning 25 different types of lashings and knots, from public speaking to camping and from learning how to forecast the weather by assessing the clouds to building a fire and cooking for your friends. Oh, those were great memories!

> CHANCE FAVOURS THE PREPARED MIND.

The biggest lesson I took was living by the Scout's motto, 'Be Prepared'. Those two words may seem profoundly simple, but they are simply profound. It is easier said than done. It can be as simple as having the consideration of taking an umbrella before going out just in case it rains to learning how to cope with life in all of its strangeness and wonder or as complicated as planning to start a business or, simply, a conversation. The success of your efforts may just hinge on your level of preparation.

Being prepared has allowed me to thrive in situations outside my comfort zone. In my teens, it allowed me to achieve good grades by taking the right actions to ensure the best results. In the army, it allowed me to pack sufficient equipment and to plan and execute various missions successfully. When I was living in London on my own, integrating into student life was easier.

Being prepared does not merely mean to do the right things. More importantly, it means having the right mind set. Mentally, you must be prepared. Only then may you also be physically prepared. I had to be mentally prepared for living in a foreign country with a different culture. I had to be prepared to be misunderstood due to my poor command in that foreign language, cultural differences, and heavy Singaporean accent! After the first year in university, I had to be prepared to work three jobs while studying full time as funds had run out and student loans (being foreign) was not an option. It was through my ability to be mentally prepared and grace that allowed me to pivot and shift my course swiftly to ensure success.

In life, there are many things that may happen that you simply cannot prepare yourself for. However, the need for mental awareness is of utmost importance. It not only allows you to live life purposefully but also allows you to experience more of life at a much higher level. 'Chance favours the Prepared Mind'. By being mentally prepared, you are able to create your own luck, or, rather, you are able to see and maximise opportunities more often than not for you are truly open to the abundance of the universe. By being prepared, you can truly live life on your terms more frequently and not let life live you.

Question: What single thought do you need to implement to allow you to see more opportunities?

"It is better to be prepared for the opportunity and not have it then to have the opportunity and not be prepared."

– Les Brown

SELF-PITY

Maisy was a beautiful lively four-year-old cream-coloured Labrador. One day, Maisy went lame on her front right leg. She was hopping on three legs before being taken to her vet. She was evidently in quite a lot of discomfort, whimpering a bit when she accidentally bore weight on her lame leg. Pain relief was prescribed then, and she was kept in relative comfort. Further investigations revealed a bone tumour in her right humerus. Thankfully, there was no evidence of tumour spread elsewhere. Her affected leg was amputated.

The surgery was uneventful, and she recovered well from the operation. She was amazingly pain-free without drugs only after a week from the surgery. Her guardian was extremely concerned whether Maisy

> LIFE IS TOO SHORT AND TIME YOU HAVE IS LUCK.

will feel sorry for herself losing her limb and only having three legs left. Considering it had not been explained to her why her leg was being removed, her guardian's concerns were understandable. They were unfounded as Maisy improved from strength to strength, was soon running and able to do everything she used to do before the lameness occurred. If you were not told, you may not even have realised she had three legs!

Animals have a remarkable way to recover or cope with their lives. There are cats with one eye, birds with no toes, and dogs with healed injuries that bounce back. They do not seem to show any self-pity. They just seem to get on with similar enthusiasm as before.

What about you? Have there been moments in your past where you felt sorry for yourself? I know I have. I felt like I needed and deserved a break from the universe. I just wanted to take a break from life and crawl into a little hole and hide. I then realised that, while I was doing that, the world goes on. The world does not stop. Time does not pause. What time was used in self-pity is forever lost. You may spend days feeling sorry for yourself, others take weeks. You may even know someone who spends his entire life feeling sorry for himself.

Self-pity does not help the situation in any way at all. It does not bring any positive value to the problem or the situation. Having self-pity only serves to make you feel like you are a victim. There is much to learn from animals where they do not feel sorry for themselves. Instead, they just accept it and continue with life the best they can. They do not spend time wondering, "Poor me," or "Why me?" They just crack on.

Strive not to be the victim, not to feel sorry for yourself, and not practice self-pity. Life is too short and time you have is luck. You are much stronger than you think. More importantly, your life is yours and you should take extreme responsibility to live an unreasonably, astounding, great life. You deserve it. Some have said, "You only live once". It should be corrected to "You only die once. You live all the time". Be sure to live with intent.

Question: Do you feel that your suffering is unique and that nobody understands you? Is that really true?

Action Tip: Do one thing that you enjoy the most and experience fully the moment you first felt the positive feeling. Hang on to that moment, burn that into your memory, and recall it when you need it again in the future.

"I never saw a wild thing feel sorry for itself. A small bird would drop frozen dead from a bough without ever feeling sorry for itself."

– D.H. Lawrence

Enjoy

LIFE AND DEATH

The front leg was shaved. A spirit swab was applied. The needle went in smoothly into the vein. Snowy, the 15-year-old Retriever, did not flinch. The sedative given to her earlier had taken effect and she was just resting with her guardian, Stella. The overdose of anaesthetic slowly circulated her body. Brave tears were streaming down her guardian's eyes. She could smell her doggy ears that were so familiar to her. Snowy looked at her guardian for the last time and her eyes glazed over. The solution had taken effect. Her heart stopped beating as Snowy leapt beyond the rainbow bridge.

Stella was recounting how she saw Snowy being born so many summers ago. They spent many years and went on countless walks together. They had fun sharing moments in health and sickness. Stella knew the end was near when Snowy was slowing down and not doing what she normally did. In the end, she had to make the hardest decision that only she could make as Snowy's guardian.

MANY PEOPLE DIE YOUNG AND ONLY GET BURIED WHEN THEY ARE MUCH OLDER. THEIR LAST BREATH WAS MERELY A FORMALITY.

With the arrival of each beautiful morning you experience, you grow closer to your end. With every single day that we live, we take one step closer to our final day. How do you live your life? You are not guaranteed a lifespan of any fixed amount. It is easy to presume that life will go on for some time, especially when you are young. It is too easy to say, "No worries, I will do that later. I have got time. No rush." It can be beyond your control, expectations, and understanding.

Life can be whimsical. Life can be fragile. How you choose to live each day is important. There is not a 'trial period' where you are preparing for living. There are no rehearsals for life. This is it.

How are you living your life? Are you balancing living like there is no tomorrow with behaving like you'll live forever? Are you allowing yourself to grow mentally and emotionally, if not physically? Or are you taking it easy, thinking you have life figured out and are now on 'auto-pilot'? Many people die young and only get buried when they are much older. Their last breath was merely a formality.

It can be very easy to cruise through life and to merely exist instead of truly living. You wake up, brush your teeth, go to work, eat food, have a chat with your family and/or friends, sleep, and repeat the events the next day. This happens daily. Before you know it, a week is gone, a month is gone, a year is gone, and just in a flash, you look back and wonder how did time pass you by like that? There are some that will say, "When such and such happens, life will be good." Or "When I have this or that, I can then get on with life." Unfortunately, it does not work like that. Life is happening every moment you take a breath. John Lennon said, "Life is what happens to you while you are making other plans." This does not imply that you have to pack your life with so many activities, that is senseless. It is merely asking if you know why you are living and also to remind you of the fragility of life. We all come with an expiration date and we do not know when it is. Are you living in a way that, if you should die now, you can clearly and definitively say, "It is ok. I have lived my life the best way I could. I have given myself as much as I could. I have done what I want to do as fully as I can. I am ready to go." What would you say or think and how would you feel if you were told that you had only one month to live? Would there be peace and a sense of fulfilment? Or would there be regrets and the 'could-have-been's, 'should-have-been's or 'what-if's?

Keep the shortness of life at the forefront of your focus. Live your life purposefully. The gift of life is precious. It is a miracle that you are created and can breathe. Be sure you propagate your genius and share your life with the world. The magic in you is so stupendous that it should be exposed and celebrated.

Snowy had a full life, completed with meaningful memories with her guardian, Stella. How are you going to feel at your end?

Question: What is the most profound positive change you can bring to those around you?

Action Tip: Exhibit and excel in your gift daily.

"When we were born, we were crying while the world rejoices. We should live our lives in such a way that, when we die, the world cries while we are rejoicing."

– Robin Sharma

PUSH HARD AND BREATHE DEEP

This is a tribute to my mother, the mother of my sons, and all the mothers in the world. What you can do and have done is nothing short of sheer astounding magic and no man can ever produce anything close to what you have achieved. I stand in awe of you. Thank you.

Lola is a three-year-old Welsh Springer Spaniel that is whelping. This is her first litter. At least three viable puppies were seen during her ultrasound scan four weeks ago. One liver and white pup was born an hour ago. That puppy is just resting beside her. The time is 1 a.m.

Lola has been in labour for the past two hours. You can see her push and strain as her hormones kicked in to contract her uterus. Her cervix is dilated and her pup desires to be separated from its mother, its creator. Her face is concentrated. Furrows on her forehead appear. Her body stiffens. After a few minutes of pushing, she relaxes. Nothing apparent is happening

{ REST IS NEEDED FOR RESULTS TO HAPPEN. }

externally. She drinks a bit of water and licks her new-born puppy. For 15 minutes, she appeared to be looking around but not really concentrating. Her breathing is controlled and relaxed. Then she starts again. The intensity increases after her rest and over the next few hours of repeating the cycles of hard pushing and deep relaxation, a total of five puppies were introduced into the world.

Sometimes, when you work towards your goals in life, when you are striving for something wonderful in your career or personal life, you will put in 110% of your effort because you know that, without hard work, you will not achieve success. You will stretch your mind, body, and soul to expand your context so success can be achieved. You think that only losers rest and relax and winners never give up (and of course, you are a winner). You may be revising harder than anyone in your studies, clocking more hours at work, or just doing your best to allow your relationship to thrive.

You push and grind relentlessly. You are determined to achieve where others have failed or perhaps just obtained mediocre results. You make sure all 't's are crossed and 'i's are dotted. You feel there is no time for rest. You have heard that what you put in is what you get out, so you put in a massive amount of effort as you desire massive results. You do not give up and you do not give in. You tell yourself and others that 'Rest is for wimps' and 'I will sleep when I am dead'. You burn out.

Life is balanced. Just like Lola, who had episodes of intense pushing and subjected her body to pressures never experienced before, she coupled that with waves of deep relaxation before she continued. She did not try to push all the puppies out in one sitting nor did she keep pushing and not stop at all. Without those regular intervals of deep rest and breathing, she would not be able to deliver five puppies into the world. Rest is needed for results to happen.

Sometimes, it is too easy to 'just keep going on'. It is too tempting to think, 'If I do not keep pushing, I will not achieve what I want to achieve'. You may not realise that the secret to high performance leading to massive results is the ability to deliver consistently high levels of performance. And to be able to do so will require the same amount and intensity of relaxation. It is a cycle that goes around. It is not a path that leads straight.

Usain Bolt's training schedule consists of more than 50% rest and not training. It is actually in the periods of rest that his muscles grow. Many breakthroughs are discovered when the mind is relaxed. You are not designed to relentlessly work. To expose your genius, you must allow your body, mind, and soul to rest. Only when you couple your High Excellence state where you produce your best work with your Deep Relaxation period, you are able to preserve your Genius.

Life is about striving and exposing your potential to the limit. However, to do so, it does not only consist of hard intense work. Remember that the same degree and intensity of rest are required too, as it will allow your potential to grow even more and produce greater results.

Question: Do you give yourself regular short breaks often and long breaks occasionally?

Action Tip: Recharge yourself by resting for 10 minutes after 60 minutes of intense work (can be creatively or physically).

"Rest well and prosper."

– Modification of Star Trek saying

TWO SIDES OF A COIN

Arthur was a three-year-old tricoloured Border Collie. His guardian described him as 'interesting' and 'contrary'. When he was with his guardian and his family, he was the soppiest, most relaxed, and happiest dog in the world. He played, barked excited woofs, and was as gentle as he could be with his two-year-old young guardian. There was no hint of viciousness, ferocity, or distrust at all.

THERE IS SO MUCH MORE TO EVERY INDIVIDUAL THAN WHAT YOU SAW OR UNDERSTOOD IN THE PAST.

However, when he went on walks and saw other people, especially when they did not have a dog with them, Arthur turned into the doggie version of Mr Hyde. He would bark from a distance and snarl if they should approach closer. It probably was the 'protective' mode you see in some breeds. He just wanted his pack safe.

So, Arthur is a dog with two personalities, depending on the situation. Have you got two personalities? Have you met someone with opposing personalities? There are polar opposites to traits in people. For every trait a person displays, she (or he) is capable of exhibiting the opposite trait to the same degree. For example, if someone is very generous usually, given the right circumstances, this person will show the same degree of stinginess. If someone appears to be nonchalant and uncaring, she (or he) can show the sensitive side under the right circumstances. The list goes on, like being disorganized and organized, sensitive and insensitive, happy and sad.

You almost wonder when a so-called 'happy' person appeared to be happy all the time, it is likely that this person might be hiding or processing some great pain and unhappiness in her life. It would be a folly to think that this person would always be happy and have no concept of sadness. Have you not been surprised before by the stingiest person in your family or workplace making the most generous of donations when needed? Or the most seemingly simple-minded person comes up with the most profound appropriate thing to say when the occasion arises? (They usually do!)

What about you? Have you surprised yourself thinking that it is not like you to do something and you find yourself doing it? Have you succeeded in something before that you never thought you ever could? Or vice versa, was there something that you knew was a sure win, a definitely completed task, something you can dig your teeth into with gusto but failed to do so because you lost interest along the way?

Perhaps you need to understand that you are not who you think you are, and neither are others. There is so much more to every individual than what you saw or understood in the past. No one ever sees every facet of another, so how can you be sure what that person is like? It is way too easy to draw conclusions about others and presume their thoughts, actions, and behaviours. If you do so, you may be surprised when unexpected results occur.

Another factor to consider is that you are capable of learning. Others are capable of learning. When you learn, you may change. You are no longer the same person. That applies to others as well. It is way too presumptuous to think you can predict an outcome based on past experiences. The past does not equate your future. You may be right, but you may also be wrong. Remember, you are not your own thoughts, and neither are others.

Perhaps what may be wise is to keep an open mind, never ASSUME (you may know the story behind that word!) anything for certain and keep the faith. Being aware and open will allow you to receive more input and results that may be surprising but because you were ready to receive, you can see them.

Remember, you may be more bi-polar than you think. (This is said with utmost respect and compassion if you have been diagnosed or have been affected by someone with bi-polar syndrome.) Understand yourself and learn to accept and love both aspects of your traits.

Me? I just make sure I have a dog with me when I meet Arthur in the park!

Question: What are your opposing traits?

Action Tip: See which traits empowers you most.

"The test of a first-rate intelligence is the ability to hold two opposed ideas in mind at the same time and still retain the ability to function."

– F Scott Fitzgerald

SEASONS OF LIFE

Nature has a wonderful way of having four purposeful seasons. In Spring, life begins a fresh start with the creeping in of the magical sun and a spark of positive energy. It is followed by Summer where it is all about maintenance and growth, basking in the heat and thriving steadily. It is harvest time in Autumn where she produces her abundance for all to see and at the same time, winding down. Next comes Winter, where life almost come to a standstill and has a well-deserved break from the hustle and bustle. It is when Nature rests on the bare minimum while preserving its internal energy for the next burst of life in Spring.

JUST LIKE LIFE CANNOT BE SUNNY PERPETUALLY, IT ALSO CAN'T RAIN ALL THE TIME.

Your life is not dissimilar. You have your seasons too. As Nature intended, you should embrace each season for it is all necessary for your growth. In your Spring, you may take up a new job, explore a new relationship, enter a new phase in your life (like parenthood!), or simply learn a new skill. It is exciting, it is fresh, it is full of possibilities and opportunities. Immerse yourself fully into this new era of your life. Absorb all the thrills and positivity. It allows you to be young again, regardless of age. Anything is possible. Life is exciting!

In your Summer, things are going well, seemingly without effort. You are thriving (even without trying) in your job, relationship, learning, and in life. Everything seems to go your way. You are contented and life is easy. Cruising becomes the norm. You cruise in everything you do. You simply cannot do wrong. Every little mistake becomes a great opportunity. You are simply enjoying life as it is.

You have your Autumn, where all the effort you have put in and the foundation you have placed is finally paying off. Your boss, team members, clients, and friends love and appreciate you. Your family understands your worth and how important you are to them and expresses that to you. Maybe your son or daughter (finally!) turns around and tells you what a great parent you are. The skill you have been practicing or the language you have been studying finally comes into practical use, allowing validation that you have invested your time wisely. Everything pays off. Opportunities appear everywhere and you see the world in its abundance. Life has never been more plentiful.

Then comes Winter. This is when things go wrong. A client complains. Your workplace environment becomes not ideal or even toxic. You fall out with your partner, possibly leading to a failed relationship. You hit a dead-end in your business, or worse still, go bankrupt. Your health is affected. You may receive a piece of terrible news. Anything and everything goes wrong or fails in all you do. Using the well-known expression 'life sucks' fundamentally. It is very common (and normal) to feel like the whole world is against you and life really hates you and does not go your way.

At this time, it is useful to remember that this is just Winter. Like all the other seasons, it soon will pass. Take this time of (seemingly) tragedy to rest and regroup yourself. Find your soul again and remind yourself of what you are internally. Accept and embrace all the feelings you are having and understand that it is all part of humanity. It is only when you experience pain and suffering that you can appreciate joy, peace, and tranquillity better. Use the pain to redefine yourself. Process the suffering to understand more about yourself. Be grateful that you have been allowed to feel what you are feeling for it clearly shows that you are indeed alive and not merely living. Pain does not affect those who exist as much as those who truly live. The more pain you feel, the more alive you are.

Know that these are nothing more than life's lessons and Spring is just around the corner. Retreat, hibernate, preserve your core but do not die (or give up). Push on because you know that, undeniably, it is just a matter of time when Spring comes. When she does, you will be ready.

Your life is like the seasons. It cannot be happy or sad all the time. Accept, embrace, and enjoy every single tear from laughter or sadness. Have faith and trust that the seasons will come and go, exactly how Nature intended it. Just like life cannot be sunny perpetually, it also can't rain all the time.

Question: Which is the season that allows you to learn and grow the most?

Action Tip: Recognize the seasons in your life and write them in your diary.

"What feels like the end of something is usually the beginning of something else."

A UNIVERSAL BANK ACCOUNT

Let's pretend that you have a bank account that has exactly £1,440 in it, no more and no less. You are allowed to draw as much as you want from this amount but there is one catch. It is that regardless of how much you draw out of it, the amount becomes ZERO at the end of the day. So, would it make sense to draw all of it (£1,440) out every day? It would certainly seem silly to leave any behind in the account at all for it will be forfeited by the end of the day.

You are in possession of this special bank account. You have 1,440 minutes in a day, no more, no less. It does not matter if you are young or old, sick or healthy, rich or poor, male or female, happy or sad, you have exactly the same bank account. So, as

> TIME IS WAY MORE VALUABLE THAN MONEY.

discussed, if it were £1,440, would you do your best to make sure that you extract every single penny out of it? Are you doing the same with your time?

You may have heard of the expression 'Time is money'. Let's consider it further … Is time really money? Are they really the same thing? Both are precious. However, you can save money, but you are not able to save time. A second gone is a second gone. You are not able to put seconds, minutes, and hours into a bank account to be used later like you do with money. You can make money, but you cannot make time. Time just occurs and passes. There is no technique or formula for making time like you have for making money. You can invest money (in a business, property, stocks, etc) to make more money but there is no investment vehicle for time to make more time.

With this in mind, it should be clear that time is not money. Time is way more valuable than money. If someone steals money from you, they can either return the money or you can make more money to replace the money stolen. But when someone steals time from you, neither they nor you can ever replace it.

You should really consider how you use this extremely precious commodity. Are you investing it wisely to seek a return from it or are you wasting it in your habits that may not serve you? Are you living life purposefully or allowing life to live you? Do you think, 'You are who you choose to become' or 'You are what happened to you'?

Are you protecting your time as your most valuable asset or are you allowing others to abuse and waste it? When people steal (waste) your time, they are stealing something even more important than the costliest property you can ever own.

Question: What would you do if you had extra time in your life?

Action Tip: Regularly block off time in your life. Schedule all appointments when possible.

"The key is in not spending time, but in investing it."

– Stephen Covey

Leadership

TAKING THE LEAD

The grey wolf stopped, raised his nose, and sniffed the air. He smelt the scent of deer. He looked back at his pack of 18 wolves, made up of several young strong females, a few juveniles, and a handful of pups. He continues his way into the depth of the forest, adopting an easy canter, and the rest of the pack followed. They followed because he is the leader of the pack. They followed because they know that he will lead the way. They followed because they know they are better off doing so than not.

In life, we always have a choice of taking the lead or being a follower. Taking the lead does not need you to be in a position of authority. You do not have to be in a position of power to be a leader. Many get confused about leadership, thinking it is something that is required when you are the boss, in charge of a department, or being in a position of power. That is erroneous thinking.

> TO LEAD IS TO INSPIRE OTHERS BY THE WAY THAT YOU LIVE.

Leadership starts within. Keeping promises to yourself, making choices, and understanding yourself are forms of leadership. If you cannot keep promises to yourself, be decisive or understand yourself, how can you do the same for others? When you lead yourself, you will improve as a person. The most important (and incidentally, basic) form of leadership is to lead yourself. Learning to make decisions, taking extreme responsibility, and committing to developing the best version of yourself are demonstrations of leadership that transcend any other forms, techniques, or titles. For when you do so, others will naturally follow. They will see how you have become the person you are, how your life is transformed, and how your leadership is serving you.

By doing so, you are not only showing them the possibility of an absolute best that they can be, you are also giving them permission to do so. Humans are creatures of habit. They like to be part of a tribe. When you show them your absolute best and become a shining beacon, you are almost telling them, "It's okay to be better. It is ok to shine. Come join me!" When you start to do so, you begin leading. You do not have to be a leader to lead. It can start as simple as perfecting your craft, developing your passion, or excelling in all you do.

When you do so, it will inspire others to follow. They may think, "Wow, So-and-so is extremely good at what she does. I want to be like her" or "He has really upped his game. I must catch up or lose out!" When this happens, you not only raise your own standards or the inspired person's standards, you are actually causing positive change by raising the world's standard on average. Without your improved brilliant input, the world's standards would not have increased. You are truly changing the world.

Consider the alternative of not taking the lead. You are the follower. You settle for what or who you are, not seeking improvements. Life is 'good and okay'. You are 'satisfied and fine' with your achievements or lack of. You are comfortable. You allow others or life to decide for you. You procrastinate and allow time to eliminate your choices and leave you with the remaining options because you are not motivated. You do not seek to delve deeper into yourself, you feel you know yourself well and 'accept' the person you think you are. Life is secure, unchanging, and easy.

At work, you follow convention and simply model after best or easiest practices to get by. You take no risk and do not do anything that has not been tried or tested. You do not push boundaries for you desire expected consequences. You do not try new things for you are afraid of failure. Your life is easy, safe, and simple. It may sound like a logical option, after all, who wants to fail?

There is only one problem. Each of us is born into genius. Sadly, most of us die in mediocrity. There is a huge difference between living and merely existing. You may be alive but are you truly living?

What would you give to catch a glimpse of a better version of yourself? Would you take a risk? What would you pay to achieve the highest level of your chosen craft? Would you invest time, effort, and energy to find out? What would you sacrifice so that all around you and the world will benefit from your magnificence? Would you take the lead?

In life, you can always choose either to be a leader or a follower. There are no right or wrong choices. They are just simply choices, with consequences.

Leadership is not a title or something only those in power or in charge can perform. To lead is to inspire others by the way that you live. To lead is to walk through the fires of your hardest times to step up into forgiveness. To lead is to remove any form of mediocrity from infiltrating the quarters of your life in a dazzling celebration of the majesty that is your birthright. To lead is to turn your terrors into triumphs and translate each of your heartbreaks into heroism. And more than all else, to lead is to be a force for good on this tiny planet of ours.

The grey wolf has chosen to lead. Regardless of your position or what you do, are you ready to take the lead now?

Question: What do you have to do to start leading?

Action Tip: Great leaders start off by being great followers. Be sure to practice following. It will teach you to lead better.

Credit: Robin Sharma

"The single best way to inspire your teammates to become the natural leaders they are meant to be is to model leadership mastery yourself."

COVID 4:

THE LEADER WITHIN

Due to government regulations during this COVID-19 pandemic, many businesses have been shut and many employees have been furloughed. For those businesses that remain open, trade is vastly affected by the curfew imposed (Not all, the supermarkets, internet businesses, and delivery services are thriving!) and those still working may be working twice as hard for half of the reward. In these situations, it can be extremely easy to be disheartened, disillusioned, disappointed, in despair, and feel like you have been robbed by something out of your control. You may throw your hands up in the air and exclaim in exasperation, "Man, why do I even try? Why is this happening to me? How can I even compete with this? It is absolutely beyond my control!"

It is true that no one could have anticipated the Coronavirus and the devastating consequences. These situations are thrown at you without warning and there are regulations that you must follow and rules that cannot be broken.

You may rely on your leaders to make decisions and form the environment that you live in. These include political leaders, industry leaders, and right down to the owner of the company you work for. Through their decisions and actions, your present situation has been constructed for you, without your permission. However, is it really true that you totally have no control? What about your thoughts? They still solely belong to you. You can control your thoughts which lead to your choices of words, feelings, and actions at all times.

There is a leader within you. You do not need a title before you can call yourself a leader. Anyone can start leading by starting with themselves. Lead from within, whether you are a leader to others or not. The world needs you to lead now as it always has done.

> EVERY TIME WE POINT A FINGER AT OTHERS, ONE FINGER POINTS OUT AND THREE OTHERS ARE POINTING BACK TOWARDS US.

Some give up control and allow others and the external environment to lead them. They allow their thoughts (which leads to speech, emotions, and actions) to be governed by other people and external factors. They become victims. The narration they tell themselves goes something like, "It's not my fault. I can't help it. I did not have a choice. I am just unfortunate and unlucky. I have a hard life. I have too much responsibility. If ... (fill in the blank) had (or hadn't) happened, my life would not be like this." There is a lot of finger-pointing (either literally or figuratively). A lot of "It's someone else's fault. It's because of some situation." Let's remind ourselves that every time we point a finger at others, one finger points out and three others are pointing back towards us.

There is another way. We can take Extreme Personal Responsibility (EPR) and look inwards for solutions. We can choose not to give the power to others or external situations that are beyond our control to depict whether we smile or not. We can elect to keep and retain the power that makes our thinking, creates feelings, and affects our mood. Why would you give this important power to others? When we take EPR, we are telling ourselves a story of leadership, not of victimhood.

To master EPR, just like any other skill, it takes practice. It takes time, effort, and work to calibrate and recalibrate our inner mindset and feelings. It is something not often taught. However, once you have fire-proofed your thoughts and battle-proofed your feelings, it is extremely difficult for external factors to bring you down.

For those whose businesses have been shut down or greatly reduced, it is time to pivot to think about how else you can serve your customers or even change the entire business plan. For those who have lost their jobs (or furloughed), use the time to improve your education and learning. This will enable you to increase your value and you will come out stronger and more useful when you return to your work or in your new job.

There are measures and actions that you can always take, despite everything else. As long as you are alive, you fight daily for who you are and who you want to become. No COVID-19, -20, -21, or any external situation can deny your existence, your uniqueness, your brilliance, and your genius. You have a choice in every moment. The door to happiness swings inwards, not outwards. All answers that you seek can be found within if you choose to lead yourself.

Question: What can you do to improve yourself if you found unexpected free time?

"Be the change you wish
to see in the world."

– Gandhi

THE UNALTERABLE, THE CHOICE,

AND THE PROMISE

When you rescue a dog, you may or may not know about his past. What you do know is that you cannot do anything about it despite how hard you try for it is the Unalterable. However, what you can do at present is to decide how you want to care for him now, what to feed, how to communicate, and where he rests. You have the Choice. In the future lays the Promise that he will develop into the best version of the dog he is. Does this sound like how you would think and the actions you would take?

Do you apply the same thinking to yourself? You have an Unalterable Past, the Choice of the Present, and the Promise of the Future. Do you live in the past, allowing it to define who you are, impeding your present actions and adversely affecting your future?

> HIDING AND BEING SMALL SERVE NO PURPOSE AT ALL.

Your unalterable past is important. It serves as experience and lessons for you to learn what worked and what did not. It allows you to have a collective knowledge of your successes and failures, a part of your life that you have lived. Everything happened for a reason. Every event had a purpose and every setback its lesson. Failure, whether of the personal, professional, or even spiritual kind, is essential to personal expansion. Never regret your past. Embrace it as the teacher that it is. Success comes through good judgement, good judgement comes through experience, and experience comes through bad judgement. There are no mistakes, only lessons. Learn from your past, do not live in it.

Your present is wondrous. It is liberating. It allows you the Choice to do what you want to do, say what you want to say, and, more importantly, think what you want to think. All your words and deeds start with your thoughts. Either you control your mind, or it controls you. What are you thinking of most of the time? The quality of your thoughts determines the quality of your life. If there is a lack in your life, it is because there is a lack in your thoughts. Practice the Attitude of Gratitude. Allow yourself to be amazing. Allow the rest of the world to see how amazing you are. Give them the gift of your being and, in doing so, you will be giving yourself the gift of the wondrous you as well. Hiding and being small serve no purpose at all. They need to see the magic of you. You need to see the magic of you. So choose your thoughts carefully. It will allow you to choose your words and deeds better.

Your future is unknown and therefore has the Promise of being whatever you want. It is only limited by the limitations in your mind. Practice creative visioneering. Lead your life with purpose. In a glimpse of an eye, as fast as a butterfly flutters its wings, your future will undoubtedly become your past. Are you being aware of time passing you by? The day to be lived next week will suddenly become your day lived last week. Have you used that day wisely? Were you even aware of that day happening or did it become a figment of your imagination of a distant past in the busyness of your day? Can you recall each day lived? Remember the time when you had an amazing day? The day you fell in love? Or became a father or a mother? Maybe you won a competition or perhaps you lost? The days that were burned so deep into your memory that, at times, you still have vivid visions of them. The days that truly evoke your emotions. Do you still have days like that? Why not?

Remember, your present self is richer than your past self for you have the currency of Choice. Your future self is richer than your past and present self for it has the currency of time and Promise. Always remember that what lies behind you and what lies in front of you is nothing when compared to what lies within you. Your actions today (not in the past) will affect your results tomorrow. Your past does not equate your future. Are you learning from your Unalterable to make great Choices that will allow the Promise of your future be yours? Balance living like there is no tomorrow with behaving like you will live forever.

Question: What lesson can you take from the past to affect the choices you make today that will lead to the future you desire?

Action Tip: Look for lessons in every bad experience you had. Realise that there are no bad lessons, only great lessons that need to be sought.

"If you are depressed, you are living in the past. If you are anxious, you are living in the future. If you are at peace, you are living in the present."

– Lao Tzu

WHY IS WHY IMPORTANT?

Watching a rat solve a puzzle to obtain its reward is fascinating. It would navigate through a maze, climb obstacles, used the surrounding objects to form a bridge to cross a gap and undo latches to get its reward.

It is interesting when the rat is placed at the start of the puzzle without reward, not much happens, she explores the puzzle with curiosity and her pace is slow and relaxed. However, when the reward (like cheese with peanut butter) is presented, you can almost see the switch turning on in the brain, the eyes light up, the movements quicken, and a source of energy and life zaps through her and her pursuit is relentless and purposeful until she obtains the reward.

KNOWING WHY IS ESSENTIAL FOR LASTING SUCCESS AND THE ABILITY TO AVOID BEING LUMPED IN WITH OTHERS.

Her actions are motivated by her 'Why'. With the reward, she now has a reason (her 'why') to move quicker, think faster, persist longer, try more methods, fail more frequently, and recover more rapidly. Her life at that moment in time is no longer just 'chilling' or 'exploring'. She is in clear pursuit of a worthy goal.

In your life, how often do you know why you are

doing something? Are your daily actions contributing to achieving your reward, your goal? (Have you got a clearly defined goal?) Or are you merely doing things the way you know, without purpose? Do you feel that time passes really quickly and, before you know it, your day has ended (usually with you feeling exhausted) or your week has ended? Do you actually know why you have been doing what you have been doing?

In life, it is crucial to convey WHY you do it more than WHAT you do. People may be attracted to you because of your WHAT, how you look, how you talk, the friends you associate with but stay with you because of WHO you are, your WHY. Knowing WHY is essential for lasting success and the ability to avoid being lumped in with others. Anybody faced with the challenge of how to differentiate themselves from others is basically a commodity, regardless of WHAT they do or HOW they do it. Would you want to be another commodity?

Knowing your 'Why' not only allows others to understand you, it also allows you to understand yourself. If you do not have a clear 'Why', not only will it confuse others, but you may also get confused about your purpose.

It can be very difficult to figure out your 'Why' for many reasons. Firstly, you may not even be aware of this concept and the importance of it and, hence, not put any energy or thought into it. Next, life can very easily take over, especially if you have children or an extremely busy life. Your 'Why' can be consumed in parenthood (especially mothers who are usually the primary carers) in just surviving each day or simply making sure you are doing the best for your children (that is also a 'why'!). Remember that your children do grow up and it is important to spend time on yourself too. There are many reasons why life may not allow you the capacity to think of your 'Why', for example, extreme circumstances, chronic debilitating illness, lack of energy, etc. However, it is in those situations that you have to hold on to your 'Why' even tighter. Lastly, you may not have experienced enough of life to find out what is important to you. It is not uncommon for some to figure out their 'Why' only in their forties or fifties. It is then they create their most amazing work.

Question: What is your compelling reason to live an unreasonable good life and be the best version of yourself?

Action Tip: Make your 'Why' about others, not yourself. It is easier (and more meaningful) to stick to it if it involves others and it is easier to give it up if it is just for yourself.

"In the absence of clearly defined goals, we become strangely loyal to performing daily trivia until we ultimately become enslaved by it."

— Bob Proctor

Success

TAKING EXTREME

PERSONAL RESPONSIBILITY

Do you how a male octopus mates with a female octopus? The female octopus is notoriously ferocious when it comes to mating. It is not uncommon for her to devour the male octopus during copulation or even before. If you thought the fairer sex was scary in the human species, think again!

There are three ways a male octopus can mate.

Method 1: He mates carelessly and gets eaten as a result.

Method 2: He can change his colour and shape to look like a female and tricks her to get close. He then sneakily mates with her before swimming away for safety. Sometimes, he gets eaten anyway.

> LIFE DOES NOT HAPPEN TO YOU. LIFE HAPPENS FOR YOU.

Method 3: He literally amputates his penis, throws it at her from a distance and swims away to safety. This is the most common method used due to its higher success rate of not being eaten!

The male octopus has taken extreme responsibility for his actions and consequences. He accepted the result of his actions of either being eaten or becoming an amputee.

In life, do you take extreme responsibility for your actions? Are you someone who chooses who you become? Or are you simply what happened to you? It is easy to blame circumstances, events, experiences, environment, and, fundamentally, anyone or anything else but you. You have heard people say, "I had a tough childhood", "I have a medical condition", "I did not have a good education", "My partner does not support my dreams", "I am too busy", "I have been disappointed too many times", "My boss is holding me back", "I am too old", "I am too young", "I have no money" and many more. Lame people blame people.

I would suggest that you do not give the power of your feelings to anyone else. First of all, no one else really wants it. Can you imagine if someone else's feelings are dependent on your actions? It would be too much responsibility to bear! And also, why would you have something as important as your feelings to be affected by external factors apart from yourself?

Perhaps you have a great unprocessed pain or sorrow in your life. Maybe you are still reeling from the anger, disbelief, indignance, and even hatred for someone or an experience you had. You are not able to move on. You feel like you are being owed something. You want payback. You want justice. You want things to be 'fair'. You cannot believe that someone would get away with what they did to you. You cannot comprehend how something that devastating could have happened to you. You are stuck and are in limbo.

The first step to moving on to fulfil the rest of your destiny (yes, you are uniquely magical, truly brilliant, and have an amazing destiny to fulfil) is by Taking Extreme Personal Responsibility. Accept and acknowledge that everything that has happened to you in your life is completely, totally, and absolutely your choice. It is not being delusional or 'being positive'. It is not saying that no one else is at fault (though assigning blame has never helped anyone). It is simply taking the first step to self-discovery, reflection, and understanding.

It is truly powerful when you start to do that. If you can do that, you will find yourself so much further ahead compared to many who fail to do so. It is simply saying to yourself, "I am in charge of my life. I am in charge of my thoughts. I may not have been able to control what happened, but I certainly can decide how I feel about it and how I am allowing it to affect me. I will embrace and learn from my past to improve my future. I will not live in my past, mistaking it for my future. I understand that in life, sometimes you win, sometimes you learn. Everything and everyone in my life, whether they brought happiness or caused grief, are lessons that Nature has provided me to grow as a person. Life does not happen to me. Life happens for me. I am grateful for my entire past, my successes, and my failings for they made me the unique special person I am today. I am truly a remarkable person!"

Once you have Taken Extreme Personal Responsibility for yourself, you will then begin to realize that all you needed to move on is found in your heart, mind, and soul. Instead of trying to change someone else or a situation, you can start by changing your thoughts, your subsequent actions, and, ultimately, your destiny. In short, you had the answers already. You only needed to take the Power back and that starts by Taking Extreme Personal Responsibility. Don't give that Power away, no one else wants it!

The octopus has chosen. How would you choose?

Question: Who do you need to forgive most so you can be free?

Action Tip: Every time you want to blame someone, catch yourself and remember that your success and happiness is an inside game.

"Lame people

blame people."

WHAT WE SAY MATTERS

"Turn off the tele, you lazy son of a b^*&h!" screeched Doris, the ten-year-old African Grey parrot as she cocked her head, eyeing me in the consult room. Her gentle-looking elderly guardians looked at me embarrassed and sheepishly explained, "We rescued her a few years ago from a couple in an abusive relationship. We didn't teach her that!" The words that continue to spew out from our feathered friend were both expletive and colourful. The only logical thing to do at that moment was to laugh and, luckily, the guardians joined me!

> YOU TELL A STORY EVERY DAY. THE PERSON THAT LISTENS MOST TO YOUR STORY IS YOURSELF.

The parrot merely copied the words that she had heard in her environment and repeated them for her own entertainment and on her own accord. Whether she understands the meaning and implication of those words remain a mystery. There are no studies (that I know of) that compare the choice of language, verbiage, or words to the physical, emotional, or psychological well-being of speaking parrots.

In humans, however, it is an entirely different matter. All of your actions are derived from your thoughts. All deeds follow thoughts. To put it simply, all your habits, actions, and results are directly affected by what goes on in your head. You have a self-image. It is simply how you see yourself. It can be extremely different to how others see you. The question is, what do you tell yourself every day about the person you think are?

Some people apologize profusely all the time. They are always saying 'Sorry' as though their lives depended on it. They are sorry when you fall down (even when you recovered well), about the food they cook (even though it is delicious), over outcomes they could not possibly affect (like the weather), when you drop something (though they are in a different room) and other matters that has absolutely nothing to do with them, and yet they are sorry. If you keep feeding the word 'Sorry' to your mind, what do you think your mind will feel and think about yourself? You will inadvertently feel sorry for yourself! Have you been around someone like that? How does that make you feel? Apologetic and sorry? Do you find yourself mirroring their actions and start saying 'sorry' as well?

Imagine another person who woke up daily and said, "I feel amazing and today is going to be a great day!" They are likely to radiate positivity, bring great energy, and refresh all around just by being there. A simple sentence like this will form the basis of his thoughts and feelings for that moment that would increase the likelihood of it actually coming through. More importantly, it makes him feel better about himself. Do you know someone like that? How do you feel being around a person like that?

You may say, "But what if I do not feel that way? I

feel stupid and false saying it". I would simply say, "How does that person who kept saying 'Sorry' feel?" He certainly felt sorry though there was no reason to. Just like how it would work for him to feel that way by simply saying the word 'sorry', you would get similar effects saying positive affirmations about yourself and your life.

You tell a story every day. The person that listens most to your story is yourself. The person whom you spent the longest with daily is looking at you in the mirror. What story are you feeding yourself? Words are such powerful tools. When you think of a word, it sits in your mind and your mind starts to digest it. When you actually say it out loud, that effect is amplified and enhanced. It becomes your mental environment. Over time, it becomes you. The quality of your life is the quality of your thoughts. Your thoughts are made up of words, the conversation you have with yourself daily.

There are over 170,000 words in the Oxford Dictionary. Choose your words wisely in all you say. Words are indeed tools. Be sure to choose powerful tools that empower you. For example, when someone says, "How are you?", the most common answers are "Fine, thank you", "Good, thank you" or "Not bad". It is almost like an autopilot response. If you listen to the verbiage and understand the meaning, it is actually horrible! Being 'fine' and 'good' is not how we want to live our lives. We want to live an amazing life! 'Not bad' is even worse. It almost implies our life is usually bad by default and today is an exception. What if you change your answer? What if you replied with "Amazing", "Fabulous!", "Never been better!".

Whether it is true or not, the feeling you will derive will feel different, a better different. Try it!

I would like to offer you three exercises. If you are not sure, just try one. If you want astounding results, do all three.

1. Every morning, when you look in the mirror, say, "I am beautiful, and I am worth it!"

2. When someone asks, "How are you?", you will reply either "Amazing" or "Never been better!" (with positive energy and gusto, of course!)

3. Tell your loved one, "I love you."

Doris's vocabulary is limited to what she is exposed to. What words do you need in your vocabulary to do what you want to do?

> **Question**: What do you need to hear the most from whom that will allow you to be a better version of yourself?
>
> **Action Tip**: Find a role model and mirror the language they use.

"Words are the clothes thoughts wear."

– Samuel Beckett

COVID 5:

THE POWER OF 'AND'

A little six-month-old Jack Russell puppy approached the 12-year-old grumpy resident Persian cat. The cat was not impressed that her pet guardian had gotten a new inquisitive bouncy pup. The pup had his eye on the cushion that the cat was lying on. He cajoles, he crawls, and he makes little whimpering noises, as though to say, "Please let me have the cushion. I am only a pup!" The Persian cat hissed and swiped the puppy's nose, albeit gently, so no blood was drawn. The Jack Russell pup jumped back and started again, bravely taking two steps forward and cautiously taking one step back. Over a few minutes of moving forward and backward (which salsa dancers will call the cha-cha-cha), the puppy miraculously managed to grovel BESIDE the Persian cat and snuggled next to her. Her face was initially shouting, "What on earth?!" before turning into a calmer state and permitted him to stay on the same cushion.

> THE POWER OF AND: DO NOT GIVE THE POWER THAT DETERMINES YOUR SUCCESS AWAY TO EXTERNAL FACTORS.

This puppy has embraced The Power of 'And'. He was feeling fearful and courageous at the same time. He was moving forwards and backwards at the same time. He held respect for the Persian cat and himself at the same time. He was conscious of what the Persian cat could do but also aware of what he wanted. And because he had embraced The Power of 'And', he succeeded.

In life, many people understand and accept the Tyranny of 'Or'. Thoughts that may play in their heads maybe, "I can either achieve this or that." "I can either be great in the process or in the details." "I can either succeed in my career or in my home life." "I can either be traditional or modern." That is fairly normal thinking.

However, a small percentage of top-performing people and companies work on a different concept. They work with understanding The Power of 'And'. They preserve their core values and stimulate change. They maintain stability and yet disrupt themselves. They remained firmly consistent and yet innovative. They practice discipline and yet drive creativity. Fundamentally, they want the cake and eat it.

Victims blame external factors for their results, outcomes, and their lives. It could be their boss, their vocation, their childhood, the country's laws, their spouse, their children, and other reasons including a strange virus. They will say that they are not able to achieve what they had set out to achieve because of those reasons. It would be because "those obstacles happened OR I would have succeeded" sort of mentality. They have succumbed to the

Tyranny of 'Or'.

For those who succeeded, their mindset would be more like, "I may have a bad boss, poor vocation, traumatized childhood, unsupportive spouse, demanding children AND I will still succeed. I do not care if there is a strange virus. It can come AND I will still succeed." They give themselves no excuses and have no desire to be a victim. Whenever any difficulty occurs, they see it as a challenge and know that their success would be more meaningful as it was achieved amidst those challenges. The fruits of their labour would taste sweeter due to the additional hardship and suffering they had to endure. They have embraced The Power of 'And'.

If you want to express your genius to the world and truly make a difference to your life and, in doing so, also make a difference to other lives, be sure to make no excuses. Do not give the power that determines your success away to external factors. Take it back and shine despite all the challenges you may face in your life. Practice to embrace The Power of 'And'. Believe that you can be a great parent AND have a great career. In the midst of the Coronavirus outbreak, you will follow the guidelines, keep healthy, AND grow more than you have ever done. For your business, you will maintain social distancing, saving human lives, AND provide the best you can, serving others.

This is a difficult time for all. The veterinary governing body had to make very difficult choices to preserve both human lives AND animals' lives. It is very easy to stay on one side of the camp saying that we should not be risking our lives to save animals OR saying we have to risk our lives saving animals. If we could only embrace The Power of 'And' in this instance, the outcome would be nothing short of spectacular. The results will not only lie in the deeds that the profession and public can see, they would also be expressed in our hearts and minds that only we can see. We would have grown with this crisis. Take care and keep safe.

Question: What opposing goals do you have? Is it really true that you cannot achieve both?

Action Tip: Search for mentors that have accomplished what you want. Find out how they did it.

Credit – Jim Collins

"The only disability in life is a bad attitude."

F.O.C.U.S. –

FOLLOW ONE COURSE UNTIL

SUCCESSFUL

Blossom, a two-year-old black and white collie, waited excitedly in an agility competition. When the whistle blew to mark the start, she dashed off to start with a winged jump, followed by a tunnel, then a teeter-totter with her handler guiding. She continued with two more winged jumps, a series of weaving poles, the A-frame, a pause table, and a wingless jump. She finished with speed and elegance, going through a collapsed tunnel, another high winged jump, and finally a tire jump.

> WITH MOBILES, IT IS NO LONGER A TOOL BUT AN ADDICTION.

There were people cheering, whistling, and waving their hands in glee and enthusiasm. Other dogs were barking in protest, excitement, and anticipation. There were flags fluttering in the wind, horns blasting at the other side of the field for other competitions and the atmosphere was electrifying. Aromas from the pop-corn maker, candy floss machine, and the burger vans were in the air. Yet, this collie did not lose focus. She was at one with her handler, her course route, and her every movement to achieve her goal. No sound, sight nor smell could distract or deter her when she was at one with her mission.

In your life, there could be plenty of distractions that has prevented you to focus and finish what you actually set out to do. It could be people, things, events, or unexpected experiences. Many would call it normal living!

In these days, the main distraction for many has largely boiled down to a single device. It is with a huge probability that it is the very object you are reading this from, your mobile phone. Mobile phones have changed vastly from the modest piece of equipment when it first came into our lives. In the 90s they were big and chunky where usually only either businessmen or gangsters had them. Then it became mainstream, smaller, and more affordable, and, with it, made more available. These days, people develop neck strain as they are usually looking down into them.

If you were an alien coming to this planet and did not know about mobile phones, you may be thinking that the mobile phone has either become an essential life-saving device that is giving constant feedback to its user by the way many people engage with it. No one looks up anymore. There is little looking into another person's eyes when walking and smiling. No one can actually sit still and take in their surroundings anymore. When waiting for a friend or an event, invariably, you will see them reaching into their pockets to pull out their phones. If you are surrounded by people now, look up and observe.

They are not allowing themselves to have the clarity of mind to think as they always feel the need to engage with something, most conveniently, their mobile phone. With such distractions, how can one ever achieve their goals? Remember the collie running the agility course with pure focus despite the distractions to achieve her goal. With mobiles, it is no longer a tool but an addiction. It may not be a drug, nicotine, or alcohol but it is hitting the same button, the dopamine-I-feel-good button. We are extremely good at doing what we feel good about. Every time you get an email, a 'like', a new 'friend' or 'follower' on social media, you get a buzz and release a bit of dopamine, a bit of 'Ah … that feels good', not unlike getting a hit from a drug, a high felt by a smoker or a sense of calm and relief experienced by someone drinking alcohol. It is an addiction, no more, no less.

The problem with this addiction is that it has not received the taboo, common understanding, and widespread acknowledgment that drugs, smoking, and alcohol have. This addiction eats into our focus, creativity, and, ultimately, freedom. Your mental bandwidth is used up even before you start to do anything creative with it. Your genius is marred by a piece of technology and the habits that you developed.

Most people will feel like a part of their body has been cut off when they lose their mobile phone. Do you feel the same way? Protect your genius, dreams, and goals from distractions and never lose focus on the bigger picture (the picture that is bigger than the screen on your mobile!)

Question: What is the worst that could happen if you do not have a mobile? What is the best that could happen instead? Is it worth it?

Action Tip:

1. To start reducing distraction from your mobile, disable all notifications apart from text message.

2. Make it a rule to check email and social media only after noon.

3. Have a no-mobile-device day once a week, maybe Sunday.

4. Notice the difference.

"Addiction to your Distraction is the Death of your Creative Production."

– Robin Sharma

DOGGONE PERSISTENCE

Alfie, a seven-year-old Springer Spaniel, walked in confidently, leading his human guardian into the consultation room. Within minutes, while the vet was chatting with his guardian, he carried his ball and set it in front of her feet. The message was clear. In the silence, he was shouting, "Ball please!" As the conversation continued and he was ignored, he was prancing around playfully, tail wagging like it's got a life of its own, astute eyes watching closely, not taking his sight of his vet's hands and her. She relented after 10 seconds and threw the ball just one metre away. Alfie jumped half a metre off the ground, spun round, dashed to the ball and brought it back to her feet within seconds. "Again!" she heard his bright eyes cry. She resisted, focusing on

> NEVER GIVE UP.
> NEVER GIVE IN.

asking his guardian the reason of the visit. Would Alfie take 'no' for an answer? Of course not! He pleaded, cajoled, teased, whined, flirted, pushed, and insisted until she gave in and threw the ball again ... and again ... and again ... and again. The persistence of Alfie is instructive.

I reflected upon myself, how often do I persist to achieve what I want and how often do I give up at the first sign of rejection and resistance? I remember how after the first year at Vet College, my father told me my college funds had ran out due to unforeseen circumstances and I had to sort out the rest of the monies needed for the next four years. I remember how I failed three times in major exams for the first, third, and final year of college. I remember the multiple times when I got rejected looking for a job. I remembered all the "No, that is impossible" I heard when I wanted to set up a vet practice. I remember the resistance I faced when I introduced new ideas to the practice. More importantly, I remember how I overcame every single obstacle listed above by not giving up.

However, I also remember the time when I failed to achieve satisfaction in a pet guardian though his pet recovered. I remember how I had let my fellow army brothers down when I failed to execute a mission properly, how I failed my exams by insufficient preparation and the challenges I gave up because it was too difficult. I remember giving up playing the guitar when my father was trying to teach me. So, I know the feeling of giving up. Though it may seem 'acceptable' at that time because of circumstances or whatever reasons (or excuses) we came up with. Over time, it does accumulate and can become a habit if we are not aware.

I think back to Alfie. His basic drive and commitment that says, "I don't care what you think of me. I don't care how stupid I look. I don't care if you ignore me. I don't care I am not getting results now. I don't care how impossible it looks. I don't care that the solution may not be obvious. I will persist on until I get the results I want." Children are not dissimilar. They are persistent, relentless, and committed to achieving their goals when they set their mind to them, especially the younger ones. I humbly and gratefully take this lesson of Persistence from Alfie and children. Every time I see a dog or a child, I reflect upon my challenges and remind myself of the persistence I have in me to demand the results I want. Never give up. Never give in.

Question: What reasons do you come up with when you give up something you thought you wanted to achieve? Were there actually reasons or excuses?

Action Tip: Find any opportunity to practise delayed gratification. Every time you feel like giving up, go one tiny step further.

"If you are going through hell, keep going."

– Winston Churchill

FEAR

A skinny mongrel peeked out from his doghouse in the shelter. He was dirty, and his coat was unkempt, possibly mangey. His eyes darted around, looking for any possible signs of threat. He crept out, hunched back, and picked on his food prepared for him in a ceramic bowl, still warily glancing around. He would jump and dash back into his house at the slightest movement or sound. His eyes, body posture, and furtive movement showed fear with no confidence evident.

Fear can cause an animal so much distress that it is not able to exhibit its normal behaviour and, at times, even elicit an abnormal response. I am reminded by the fear that we possess in us.

IMAGINE WHAT YOU COULD ACCOMPLISH AND ACHIEVE IN YOUR LIFE IF YOU HAD NO FEAR.

A baby is born with two fears: loud noises and falling. Almost all other fears are learned. What fears do you possess? The times when you felt you should have done something, but you were held back; was it rationale or was it fear? Common fears include making the wrong decision, making the right decision, doing something for the first time, looking silly, being laughed at, losing credibility, failing, succeeding, getting it wrong, losing someone, and many more.

Fear is the ultimate mind killer. When you fear, it cripples your ability to exercise your mental faculties to the maximum. You hesitate or hold back. Some fears are rationale and protective, like not putting your hand in the fire in fear that it would get burnt or not wanting to gamble in fear of losing all your money. One could say that that could be making a calculated decision based on past experiences or 'common sense'. However, the fear of making the leap perhaps into a new love, a new career, a new skill, or simply just expanding your thoughts, your goals, redefining what you want to live your life for, moving on from a death of a close one evokes a different response. I am referring to the fear that stops you being more than you presently are.

What if you had no fear? Imagine what you could accomplish and achieve in your life. Many have thought and advised, "Don't dream too big. You may not achieve it and you don't want to be a failure and laughed at, would you?" or (I love this one!) "Be realistic. Be practical. Who do you think you are? Dream of and plan for something more achievable." The problem is that you can usually achieve it!

Fear is simply False Expectations Appearing Real. It is all in our mind. At this point, remember that being courageous is not the absence of fear. Showing courage is doing what needs to be done DESPITE the fear because it is the right thing to do. It is saying, "I feel the fear, but I do it anyway!"

A survey conducted in a hospice documented the biggest regrets of people at the end of their lives. Not living their dreams and not taking more risks ranked in the top five regrets (together with not spending more time with loved ones, not being more loving to their family, and not being a better spouse, parent, and child). They mentioned that it was fear that held them back from living their dreams and taking enough risks. It seemed insane not to learn from these great teachers who have lived their lives.

Embrace your inner souls. Remember that you were only born with two fears (and to be fair, many have conquered those fears anyway!) and the rest are learnt. Be brave and courageous to live the life you have and want. The Spanish say, "A life lived in fear is a life half lived." Live your lives to the fullest so you may look back and say, "I lived a purposeful life. I felt the fear, but I did it anyway."

Question: What is your greatest fear?

"The greatest mistake we make is living in constant fear that we will make one."

– John C Maxwell

THE OPPOSITE OF SUCCESS

IS NOT FAILURE

In veterinary pathology, preparing a blood smear is done from time to time. It is when a drop of blood is placed on a microscopic slide and a special sliding technique using another slide is used to smear the drop to spread the sample across. This technique was often the bane and cause of frustration of many vets and nurses when it was first introduced and taught. It required finesse, practice, technique, persistence, and also improving upon failed attempts.

> YOU SHOULD UNDERSTAND, ACCEPT AND REMEMBER THAT SUCCESS HAS A PRICE. FIND OUT EXACTLY WHAT IT IS AND GET BUSY PAYING IT (BY FAILING).

There are similar situations that are encountered often in veterinary work like pet guardians training recall or 'heel' for their dogs, animal handling by assistants for blood sampling or minor procedures, and maybe as 'simple' as providing great consistent customer care. It is easy not to get it right the first time. The way failure is viewed really marks the end result for a person. If you viewed it as terminal or brought about the feeling of inadequacy or any negative feeling at all, it is often you would give up and accept defeat.

If you viewed it as a learning curve and one can profit from failure, you tend to succeed. You see failure in a different way. You know that no one gets it right the first time. You are not a perfectionist. You understand that if you fall down nine times, as long as you get up ten times, you will still end up standing. You realise that the opposite of success is not failure. It is simply not trying.

I remember failing three times in major exams in Vet College, in the first, third, and final year. I graduated four months later than everyone (bar a few who joined me!). It did not make me any less of a vet. In fact, looking back at my counterparts now, I see some of those who did very well have actually given up vetting due to various reasons and yet, here I am, loving every moment of it.

Success, on the other hand, is actually an extremely poor teacher compared to failure. Consider when you succeed, what do you learn? Maybe that hard work pays off or luck may be involved? You may feel good inside for a bit, given a sense of accomplishment or validation that you are worthy of the goal? Either which, the feeling does not really last, and it does not really improve you.

However, failure is a fantastic teacher. It teaches you to improve. It teaches you to achieve greater results. It forces you to face the facts that what you felt was good enough actually was not. It teaches you to be humble. It pulls out more from you. It keeps you on the edge, making you uncomfortable (comfort is the enemy of growth) and in doing so, allows you a chance to grow.

In fact, you should embrace failure as it is a direct step towards success. When you first learn how to ride a bike, you wobble and fall before learning how to keep your balance and cycle. The surest way of not falling is not getting on the bike in the first place. So, for someone not to fail simply means that person is not really pushing out of his comfort zone and learning.

Another way to look at it is if you need to fall down say, on average of 50 times, before mastering how to ride a bike, you should get excited about falling down (failing) for it surely means that you are just that one step closer to properly cycling (success). You should understand, accept, and remember that success has a price. Find out exactly what it is and get busy paying it (by failing).

The difference between someone who succeeds or fails lies in the interpretation of failing. A successful person would view it as temporary defeat and profit from failure by learning from each failed experience. An unsuccessful person would view it as a reflection of his inadequacy and accept that result as permanent. Remember that, in life, sometimes you win, sometimes you learn.

If you have been trying and have not succeeded, don't give up. Keep pushing and success will surely follow. You are not alone.

Question: What do you need at present to allow you to succeed?

Action Tip: Speak to others who have succeed in what you want to do and ask them about their stories, including their temporary defeats.

"Success is the ability to go from one failure to another with no loss of enthusiasm."

– Winston Churchill

TAKING A STAND

There are all sorts of pet guardians. Some keep dogs, some like cats. Some prefer reptiles and others prefer horses. Even simply for dog guardians, some like Staffies and others love Dalmatians. All of them share the same undeniable love for animals and yet they are all different for the various species they chose.

Yes, they chose ... They have chosen what animals to love and take care of. They made choices that include some and exclude others. Is that not very similar to how you should be approaching people and approaching yourself?

In life, there is a tendency to want to please everyone. You like to be known as 'friendly' and 'nice' and strive not to upset others. Do you realise how difficult and superficial that can be?! Many people like to have many friends. They like to please everyone. They shift their beliefs and attitudes to suit others. They try to fit in. It is entirely understandable. As a species, humans are tribal. You went through that in school, trying to fit in with friends. As you grow older, you try to fit into society. It was what everyone was doing, and

> YOU DO NOT REALISE THAT PEOPLE SPEND A TREMENDOUS AMOUNT OF ENERGY TRYING TO BE 'NORMAL'.

nobody likes to stick out like a sore thumb. Are you able to relate?

Many businesses are similar. They want to obtain 'market share'. They try to make their products and services suit everyone. They want to please all prospects. They want to be everything to everyone. They want to be as flexible as possible to make sure everyone is happy. Is that the right approach?

In life, you should be listening to yourself very carefully and understand what beliefs you have, what you stand for, and what your core is. When you have found that, you should have the strength, courage, and commitment to live the way you want to. You make friends according to what serves you best and not to 'fit in'. If everyone is your friend, no one is your friend.

In business, you should be very clear why your products and services exist and, more specifically, who is it for. You should be asking yourself, very clearly, who is going to benefit the most out of your business and get busy serving those needs. It is by doing so that you can focus on your strengths, not get distracted trying to serve everyone, and bring the most value for your intended customers. If everyone is your customer, no one is your customer. You should not be afraid to tell those who do not fit into your customer profile that it may not be a good fit, just like a bad date.

Just like pet guardians who know specifically which pet to go for and bring the best value to that individual animal, you can learn to do the same in your life and business. Be brave enough to take a stand and be yourself. You do not realise that people spend a tremendous amount of energy trying to be 'normal'.

I may not have the formula to happiness, but I know the surest way to be unhappy is to make everyone else happy. Try it out yourself and find out!

Question: What could you achieve if you stop making everyone around you happy?

Action Tip: Keep your self-esteem in check. If it is healthy, you would not need to make everyone else happy. Remember the most important person to you is you. Serve yourself well so you can serve others better.

Be yourself. Everyone else
is already taken."

– Oscar Wilde

CO-OPERATION, NOT ISOLATION

In prehistoric times, cavemen would huddle together for warmth, hunt in teams, and live in groups. They knew that strength laid in numbers. Together, they were able to increase the level of success and survivability. They were more likely to be able to hunt effectively, keep warmer by building a fire together, expand their family and, literally, live longer by being in a group. In fact, the worst thing that could happen to someone was to be banished from his or her clan. The likelihood of that individual surviving was very low.

> JOY AMPLIFIES WHEN SHARED.

In the modern society, it is no different. However, you may choose to live in isolation. It does not necessarily mean that you live alone without anyone else in your life.

In the UK, a phrase that is often heard as a form of greeting is "Alright?" You can hear it everywhere. Invariably, the answer is (99% of the time), "Fine", "Good" or "Alright" without really meaning it. It is almost like an automatic response. This is really a horrible question. It is almost like you are being lazy and not caring when you ask that for you already know the answer and you are just 'being polite' and 'normal'.

I was referring to 'emotional isolation'. It means that you chose not to share your emotions with others.

Sometimes, you pretend to be happy and that nothing is wrong, but you are crying inside. Other times, you actually isolate yourself from others and passively (or actively) avoid your friends and family.

There can be many reasons why this happened. It might be that you were taught to be resilient and have to 'deal with problems yourself'. Perhaps you perceived you were being 'considerate' by not troubling others with your problems. Maybe you thought that others would not care. Or you felt you did not deserve to have your emotions shared. The most destructive of all is when you think you deserve to be sad and miserable, and happiness was not meant for you. Usually, there is a degree of low and unhealthy self-esteem.

It is of paramount importance for personal growth to be able to express your emotions. When you are happy, you love to share it. It is incredibly hard to hide your happiness and ecstasy. Can you remember an occasion when you felt amazing and tried to hide it? It does not really work! People see it instantly or, if you are indeed good at hiding, you will feel so uncomfortable inside! Recall the last time you received good news. The chances were that you were bursting to tell someone else to share it. Joy amplifies when shared. Likewise, when you feel miserable inside and you are not able to share it, it is tough. It is so tough. Your face shows hidden pain. Your heart crumbles inside and your soul is longing for a warm hug.

You need to be able to share your emotions. Many pet guardians will understand this, and they know they have an outlet for their feelings. They talk to their pets! Pets are wonderful companions in so many ways. Not only do they fulfil you physically and mentally, they also fulfil you emotionally. I remember talking to my dogs for hours about my feelings. Long conversations took place after my relationships broke down, when I passed my exams, when I got into Vet College, and so many other life experiences. I am sure if you owned a pet, you would be nodding your head in agreement, smiling a knowing smile.

It is important not to be in isolation. In the current day and age of technology, where texting is replacing conversations, Instagram is replacing meetings, the need for effective communication and sharing true emotions are even more crucial.

That is why the veterinary profession is so amazing as it does not merely treat the medical diseases of pets, it also maintains, embraces, celebrates, and returns the special unique bond between your pet and you. Working and understanding pet guardians allow sharing a bit of your vet's personality such that your relationship extends further than just being transactional.

Strive to reach out to at least one person in your life daily and truly ask with utmost sincerity and the burning desire to find out, "How are you today?" and actually genuinely listen with care because you are capable of so much better than "Alright?"

Question: What other question can you ask to receive a different answer?

Action Tip: Actually plan to allow more time for the recipient to answer your greeting so you will not feel rushed when she actually replies with her story.

"No man is an island."

– John Donne

THE RAZOR EDGE BETWEEN

SUCCESS AND FAILURE

Just to share a bit of tricks of the trade when handling animals ... Very often, the closer we handle the dangerous bits of the animals, the safer it is. For example, if you are standing literally beside the horse's back leg, it is harder to get kicked. To prevent the dog from biting you or anyone else when performing minor procedures like blood sampling and placing an intravenous catheter, the closer you get to the head/muzzle area to secure it, the less likely anyone will be get bitten when the dog swings round. Similarly, for cats, to reduce the risk of getting bitten, you place

> THE OPPOSITE OF
> SUCCESS IS NOT
> TRYING.

your hand closer rather than further away from the head. Another great example would be handling snakes. Notice how the handler always keeps her hand just behind the head and not in the middle of the body. In doing so, the snake is less likely to bite her compared to if she handled the middle part of the body as part of the restraint.

So, what is my point? It is just to remind us that true success is very similar. Just when you feel you have failed, the tide turns. Sometimes it is only when you think you cannot give any more and feel like giving up, your 'luck' changes. Success lies in the razor edge of failure. The question you need to ask yourself is not how to succeed but when you fail, do you fail forwards or backwards? Do you embrace failing or are you afraid to fail? Many would just stop trying in fear of failing. In doing so, they do not fail but they not give themselves the chance to succeed. In reality, it is impossible to live without failing at something, unless you live so cautiously that you might as well not lived at all – in which case, you fail by default.

They do not realise that the opposite of success is not failure. The opposite of success is not trying. If you did not fail, it merely meant you have not tried anything new and not expanded yourself which also meant you were not growing. When you take a close look at success you soon discover that there is a fine line that separates it from failure. It only takes a moment of decision and action.

So, if you are pushing, keep pushing! Remember, success is just on the other side of failure. Just like the paradox of the safest spot being beside the dangerous teeth or hooves of animals!

Question: What decision can you make today that will change your destiny?

Action Tip: Decide between your fear of failing and desire for success. The one that evokes the stronger emotion will win.